Beyond Survival

Beyond Survival

by

Elwood McQuaid

MOODY PRESS
CHICAGO

ISBN 0-8024-2560-7

Printed in the United States of America

When my father and my mother forsake me, the LORD will take me up.

Psalm 27:10

Note

Names, including that of the principal character in this book, have been changed. People and events depicted throughout this biography are real.

Contents

Introduction

This is the biography of a man who, like his nation, Israel, defies explanation apart from God. His story, in the early stages, is reminiscent of the book of Esther in the Bible—God is not consciously represented, yet He is obviously present and at work.

You will recognize, as the story unfolds, that people and events touch Zvi's life at strategic points in ways that cannot be coincidental. Over the tortuous course he followed in his flight for survival, you will discern a clear pattern of divine provision.

Unlike many of the stories we are confronted by today, this true-life epic has a satisfying climax. Zvi's life is far from over, of course, but the issue has been settled. He is alive today and living a joyfully triumphant life in the land of his fathers.

How he survived the Holocaust, found his way to the shores of Israel, and faced his life-transforming encounter with the Messiah is a story one can ill afford to pass by. A careful study of that life is a revelation of the lengths to which a loving Lord will go to bring one soul safely home.

Elwood McQuaid

1

Now You Are a Man

He stood at the window looking out for a long time. In the courtyard below he could see small children playing games. The gate through which his mother had left the orphanage seemed disproportionately large against the gathering darkness. At ten years of age, Henryk Weichert found himself alone. He did not know why. Nor could this frail Jewish lad begin to comprehend the maelstrom of carnage and outrage into which he and Europe were passing. The Poland a carefree child had known was gone. It would never be the same again—Adolph Hitler and his manic delusions would see to that.

Prior to 1939, Warsaw had been a happy place for a young boy to grow up. Oh, there had been guarded conversations among adults and occasional talk of war, but in the world of a small child such things meant very little. Then the Germans came and introduced Henryk to Hitler's demented world.

After awhile, an attendant came and led the boy down a long corridor to the room he would occupy with other parentless children. He slowly placed into the drawer assigned to him the few belongings he had brought. Henryk then walked to his sleeping cot and sat down. Thoughts of the recent frantic weeks rushed through his head in confused patterns. A child's mind could not assimilate the great changes that were taking place—changes that would menace the world and alter the face of Europe.

For months Hitler had attempted to use political sleight of hand to veil his true designs for Poland from the French and British. He hoped to lull them into inaction at least long enough to implement his program for armed annexation.

On August 23, 1939, the German Fuhrer announced the signing of a nonaggression pact with Russia. A secret clause in that agreement called for the partition of Poland by the two predator nations. The Vistula, Narew, and Sans Rivers would be the dividing lines between the occupying forces.

September's first days saw German panzer divisions streaming across the border. Luftwaffe aircraft simultaneously devastated Polish cities from the skies. The Polish people were determined to resist the onslaught, but their efforts could not stay the German advance. By September 9, the Fourth Panzer Division was positioned on the outskirts of Warsaw preparing to enter the city. A counterattack by Polish forces briefly forestalled the inevitable, but the weight of German armor and continuous assaults by dive bombers eventually prevailed.

On September 27, Warsaw surrendered and effective resistance was crushed throughout the country. Poland became a slave state, bled jointly by Nazis and Communists.

Hitler's plan for Poland called for annexing a portion of the country outright and forging it into the Reich as a part of Germany proper. A second area, which included Warsaw, Cracow, and Lubin, would be incorporated under German administration as the Generalgovernment. Hitler's long-range program would place the sword of aggression firmly in the back of his Russian comrades (June 22, 1941), and hopefully extend the Nazi utopia to Moscow and the hinterlands beyond.

Henryk remembered a recent afternoon when he had entered his home in the suburbs of Warsaw. Despite the concentrated bombing of the city, the area in which the Weicherts lived bore no obvious marks of war. The tree-shaded street, now taking on the colors of fall, was deceptively calm. The serenity was broken when the boy entered the kitchen and found both of his parents in tears.

"What is wrong?" Henryk asked.

"We have lost the war," his father replied. "The Germans have come to Warsaw. Go sit in the other room. I must talk to your mother."

He entered an adjacent room and sat down with his three elder brothers and sister. The air seemed heavy as he listened to the hushed conversation that passed between the boys. Arthur, the eldest, was telling them about the things he had heard from some neighbors earlier in the day. Tanks by the hundreds, and soldiers, too many to count, had come into Warsaw. Many people had been killed. Everywhere there was fear about what would happen next. They must prepare for the worst.

Mendel and Ruth Weichert were strong people. He was a quiet, reserved sort of man who was seldom known to display his emotions. Today it was different. As he tried to explain the current situation to the children, he found it necessary to pause frequently in order to regain his composure.

"Life will be changed for us now," he said solemnly. "You will no longer be free to come and go as you once did. From now on, stay close to home. If you should see German soldiers, get out of their way. We can only hope that they will soon be driven from our land. Until then, we must be strong."

At that time they could not begin to realize just how strong they would have to be. Poland and her people were entering a period of trauma that seldom had been equalled on this planet. Hitler's carefully concocted scheme for the "Aryanization" of Europe would be pursued with rabid dedication. Those who did not fit into the mold were doomed.

The Nazi program for the conquered Poles was direct and brutal. Thousands were summarily executed. Thousands more were sent to Germany to join the slave labor force. Others were ousted from their lands in the annexed territory to make way for settlers being transported to the area from Germany. Displaced farmers and other "undesirables" were forcibly deported into the Generalgovernment area, which was initially viewed by the Germans as a dumping ground for deportees. Consequently, the population of Warsaw would be swelled by the tide of refugees coming into the city. Already crippled by the ravages of war, she was ill-prepared to face the challenge of resettling large numbers of people.

Hard on the heels of the soldiers came a dreaded breed of political police known as the *Einstzgruppen*. Their function was to serve as a strike force dedicated to hunting

17

down and eliminating people who were suspected of being disloyal to the ideals of National Socialism. A reign of fear quickly spread across the country. Thereafter, the population was immersed in a perpetual cloud of anxiety, suspicion, and terror.

The pursuit of life in Warsaw became a grim business. Everywhere one went he saw scowling, helmeted conscripts of the Third Reich. It was soon evident that physical survival would be the primary occupation of the victims of the Nazi conquest. News of arrests and the imprisonment of officials soon became routine information. Neighbors suddenly disappeared without notice or explanation. Then, as if those indignities were not enough, hunger began to plague the inhabitants.

A situation that was bad for the average Polish citizen became insufferable for the members of the Jewish community. They were marked to be special objects of Nazi enmity. Hitler's charted course for "a final solution of the Jewish problem" would move through successive stages. First, Jews were to be isolated and vilified. Identifying armbands were required for Jewish citizens. Movements by Jews were restricted and their properties and persons subject to seizure at a moment's whim. Synagogues were destroyed and thousands of executions carried out. Jews were not allowed to have as much food as their Polish neighbors. Shopkeepers were dragged from their stores and beaten in the streets. Windows were broken and anti-Jewish slogans plastered on the walls of buildings. Jewish girls and women became the objects of public humiliation. Consequently, they kept more and more to their homes.

After several months of calculated harassment, Jews were forced to move into specially constructed ghetto areas. Streets were cordoned off and later walled, with Jews penned up inside. The first such ghetto was built in Lodz in May, 1940. Warsaw received her infamous counterpart in November of the same year. Ghettos often contained small industrial units through which inhabitants were expected to contribute to the war effort while being systematically starved to death.

The final step on Hitler's road to a Jewless world involved the establishment of death camps and the destruction of the ghettos. It was to be the terminal phase. Six annihilation centers dotted the area Poland had occupied prior to the war. Auschwitz, Belzec, Treblinka, and the other camps received what seemed to be an endless line of wasted Jews who filed off the boxcars and through the gates for "processing." By mid 1942, at Treblinka alone, more than 300,000 Jewish people had made the one-way trip to the incinerators.

Destruction of the ghettos began late in 1942. The enclave at Warsaw came under fire in April, 1943. There beleaguered Jews, many little more than boys and girls, mounted a heroic resistance effort. They somehow managed to stave off their hated tormentors for six weeks. On May 10, 1943 the futile struggle ended; the ghetto was destroyed.

Before the war began, 3,300,000 Jews made Poland their home. By the end of the war, three million had perished.

Those events cast the cauldron into which little Henryk and his family were thrown.

The first rude intrusion into their lives entered when a black-booted representative of the new regime called at the Weichert home one winter afternoon. After a crisp introduction, the man stated his business. "On Monday morning you will bring your three eldest sons to the railroad station in Warsaw. They will be taken to Germany for training, then put to work in an industrial plant.

"You needn't worry about them, they will be well treated. When the war is over, you will see them again."

There was no time for discussion or rebuttal. The matter had been settled by the authorities. Arthur, Hersh, and Jacob would be taken from their midst to serve their captors.

A pall of apprehension hung over the household for the remainder of the week. It was as if the family were grasping some precious thing that was irretrievably slipping from their fingers. The Weicherts seemed to be well aware of the fact that what they had known all of their lives was passing from them. Would they ever be together again? It was a question over which none of them had control.

Monday was a dismal day. The weather was bad, the mood depressing. Arthur made a few feeble attempts to cheer the family spirit. It was a vain effort.

The depot was teeming with activity. People were jammed into the terminal, jostling their way to or from the trains. Dozens of families, many of whom were friends or acquaintances of the Weicherts, had come on the same mission. Teenaged boys stood, bags in hand, ready to be ushered aboard the train for the long ride to Germany. Tema and Henryk clutched their parents' clothing during the tearful farewells. Then the boys were aboard the train and gone.

Henryk thought the house seemed larger without his brothers; it was certainly a quieter place. He and his sister now spent more time playing with one another and the neighborhood children than they had before. After a time most of the older boys had disappeared from the community, and only the small ones remained.

In the months that followed, Mendel increasingly spent long periods of time locked in silence. When the children spoke to him, the words did not appear to penetrate. It seemed that his thoughts were as far away as Henryk's brothers. When he came home in the evenings, he and Ruth would send the children into another part of the house while they talked quietly. It seemed like hours would pass before Tema and Henryk were allowed into the room. Frequently, following those conversations, Ruth wore a worried expression. The children could often see that she had been weeping.

One night the news was unusually bad. Mendel told his wife that the rumors they had heard were now confirmed. All Jewish families would be relocated within a designated area in the city of Warsaw. Notification of the order would soon come officially.

"But what will become of our home?" a distraught Ruth asked.

"It will be used for housing German soldiers. At least that is what I'm told they plan to do with most of the dwellings confiscated from Jews."

"And the children, Mendel. What will become of our children?" Her tone carried a pleading burst of consternation that had been building for months.

"I have been giving much thought to that question," her husband replied softly. "Tema must come with us. But I see no future in the ghetto for Henryk. I feel it would be best to do what we can to conceal his identity as a Jew and place him in an orphanage."

Ruth was stunned but receptive. "I've seen what has happened to the others. It can't be worse for him in an orphanage. At least we will be in the same city. Perhaps this way he has a chance."

So the decision was made. In a few days Ruth would take the boy to a home for orphans.

A mother and her son walked hand in hand through the streets of Warsaw. Ruth proceeded hesitantly, a small valise in her left hand. Somehow she wished they could walk past the orphanage into a world free from death and trouble. But it was not to be. Soon an austere gray building that stood behind a low stone wall appeared before them. Ruth quickened the pace as they passed the gate and climbed the steps toward the entrance.

Inside there was a brief exchange of introductions before the committal papers were filled out. Ruth asked for a few moments to be alone with her son. She sat down in a chair and pulled him close to her face. One hand gripped his arm tightly; the fingers of the other passed repeatedly through his hair.

Henryk looked into his mother's countenance. What he saw there would remain etched in his memory for life. She appeared to be much older than she looked just weeks ago. Her eyes were possessed by a strange, frightened expression he had never seen in them before. Still she was, to him, a very beautiful woman. Small, blonde, and round faced, she represented all that a mother could properly personify to a son. When he looked at her, he saw all the affection, strength, and attention a boy could ever desire.

She spoke in carefully measured tones. "Henryk, I want you to make a promise, one that you must always carry with you—a promise you must never forget. Do not tell anyone that you are a Jew."

"But Mother, why?"

"Because they don't like Jews here. You must watch your words. Be careful what you say, and always remember what I have told you.

"My son, you must learn to be strong. From now on you are no longer my child— now you are a man."

He could feel her body quiver as she embraced him. Rising quickly, she paused for a moment to assure him. "Remember, be strong. I will come often to see you." Then turning away, she left the room. When he could no longer hear her footsteps in the hallway, he walked to the window and looked out. He saw his mother cross the courtyard and pass through the gate.

For a time Henryk would spend hours at the window watching for his mother to come and visit him—or better still, to take him home and put an end to this bad dream. On holidays and weekends he would search the faces of those who came to see relatives, eagerly hoping to find someone who was familiar to him. But it was always the same; a disappointed boy would return to his room to await another day, in the hope that it would bring his mother back to him. By this time, however, his parents, along with other Jewish families, were enduring the rigors of their trial.

Soon things at the orphanage began to change. German teachers came to the school to instruct the children in the German language. Along with their studies in German, they were carefully exposed to Nazi political indoctrination. These youngsters were prime prospects for the Hitler youth movement being developed by the Nazis in Poland. Before long the children found themselves joining heartily in the songs of the "Fatherland," many of which were filled with anti-Jewish lyrics. Children could often be seen in the courtyard imitating the goose step of the soldiers of the Reich and raising stiffened arms in salutes to the Fuhrer. After a full year of concentrated brainwashing, the boys had literally become very German. Henryk was no exception. He was now conversant in the German language and harbored the common ambition to become a soldier and fight for Deutschland.

The announcement was made at a special assembly: "You will be happy to know that you are going to take a long journey. Tomorrow morning you will board a train bound for Berlin. For the first time you will see the Fatherland. Along the way you will tour the country and get a good look at the land of the Fuhrer. Who knows? You may even see him."

Everyone was ecstatic over the news. To ride a train so far! It was the opportunity of a lifetime. And to go to Germany—What more could one ask?

Henryk was not so sure. That would mean leaving Warsaw. If his mother should come for him, he would be gone. He was disturbed even more when he learned that after their departure, the orphanage would be closed permanently. How could she find him if he went so far away? He didn't sleep much that night. His mother's words kept running through his mind: "Be strong . . . I will come back to see you." There in the darkness of the room, it seemed as though he could reach out and touch her face. He was almost certain he could feel the grip of her hand on his arm. Surely she would come for him! Finally sleep enveloped little Henryk and brought quiet to his troubled mind.

In the morning he came to a decision: what would be, would be. Germany lay ahead of him. He would go there as a man—he would be strong.

Several days on the rails provided plenty of mental diversion for the boy traveler. The countryside was beautiful. Deep ravines, with their picturesque rambling streams, passed frequently beneath the wheels of the train. It went through hamlets and cities, where people always seemed to be in a great hurry to get where they were going. And always there were soldiers. Sometimes they were strung out in long columns, marching along the roads. At every railroad station Henryk could see them walking slowly, with rifles strung over their shoulders.

The Germans kept their promise to show these Polish boys the heartland of the Third Reich. The train rumbled through many of the major cities in eastern and southern Germany. Dresden, Frankfort on the Oder, Stargart, and Brandenburg all moved slowly past the windows of the train before it swung north toward its final destination. As the train approached the city of Berlin, it slowed and moved onto a siding near a railroad station. "Everybody out!" cried one of the men who accompanied the boys. "Take all your belongings. Leave nothing on the train."

It was good to be off the train and out in the fresh air again. They waited for about thirty minutes before a gleaming black car drove up to the station house and stopped. Several uniformed Germans got out and approached the man who was in charge of the children. "Move them inside and line them up according to size," one of the officers ordered.

The boys were herded into a large room and lined up. An officer stepped forward to address the group.

"Welcome to the Fatherland. I bring you greetings in the name of the Fuhrer.

"Your group will now be divided into two units. Those who are largest and strongest will be placed in a group that will proceed to Berlin. The rest of you will return to Poland."

The soldiers then hustled them through a line where the final selection was being made. Henryk found himself standing before an angular officer.

"Well, young man, what do you want to be when you are grown?" the soldier asked.

"I want to be an officer in the German

army and fight for Deutschland," Henryk replied.

The German threw back his head and laughed. "Such courage in one so small," he said.

"But I am not too small to fight! You will see," the boy challenged.

The officer smiled down at him. "Yes, you will fight, but not now. You are too small. Go back to Poland and drink as much milk as you can. Then you will come back and serve the Reich."

Tickets and food rations were issued to those who were not selected to continue. Soon they were on the train for the return trip to Poland. For Henryk it was a great disappointment, but being a bit too small probably saved his life.

Henryk did some hard thinking on the journey home. What would he do now? He could not return to the orphanage. But where would he go? More than ever, he wanted to see his family. That was it! If his parents could not come to him, he would go to them. He would return to Warsaw and go back to his home.

It took some time to find the old neighborhood. Things had changed. As Henryk neared his home, however, surroundings appeared reassuringly familiar. Finally the homeplace came into view. He began to run excitedly toward the house. At long last, there would be a reunion with his parents and Tema. How good it was to be home again!

As he turned onto the walkway to his house, the front door opened and a woman stepped out. It was not his mother. This woman wore a German uniform. She stood before him on the sidewalk with a frozen expression. "What do you want?" she snapped. "If it's food you are after, you will find none here. Go away."

A stunned eleven-year-old spun on his heel and walked quickly into the street. Once he was beyond the woman's view, he stopped. Fresh questions now flooded his mind. What, he wondered, could have happened? Where were his parents? Would he ever see them again? How could he find them?

As he struggled with his thoughts, a boy walked toward him. Henryk paid little attention to him at first. But then he realized that the lad was Janusz, a neighbor with whom he had spent many hours at play before his days at the orphanage. Henryk called out to him and rushed forward. The boy's face registered instant recognition, but as quickly his features became rigid with fear. The youth quickened his pace and brushed by without a word. As Henryk turned to pursue him, the boy turned in at his house, slamming the door behind him.

Small fists frantically assailed the door through which the former playmate had darted. He had to find the answer. Someone must tell him where his parents had gone. At last the door opened a crack and Henryk recognized the boy's father. Before he could say a word, the man was speaking. "Go away from this place, please, go quickly."

By now the boy was weeping openly. "But why? What has happened?"

There was a brief silence. Then the door was thrown open and the man stepped out. His eyes were apprehensive as they swept the street. Pushing Henryk inside, he said: "All right, I will tell you where they are, but then you must go. The Germans have forbidden us to take Jews into our homes. To do so means death for the whole family. Even to speak to you places me in grave danger.

"Your family has been taken to the ghetto. There are no more Jews living in this neighborhood. I will tell you a place where you might find them—it is in the Jewish quarter. The wall outside is heavily guarded. I don't know if you will be able to get in.

"Now come, leave by the back door. Hurry! Tell no one you were here."

2

Like a Cat
On the Wall

Darkness was falling by the time Henryk reached the ghetto. Janusz's father had been right. Guards wearing heavy military coats that nearly dragged the ground were stationed at frequent intervals along the wall. As he stood pondering the problem of entry, several shadowy forms moved into the alley he had chosen for an observation post. Their approach startled him at first, but as they neared he could see they were boys about his own age. They came abreast of him and stopped. One of the boys, with a sturdy frame and close-cropped hair, asked what he was doing there.

"I'm looking for a way to get into the ghetto," Henryk replied.

"And why do you want to get inside? There is only death and misery beyond that wall."

Henryk responded, "I have come with a

message for some friends of my parents. But there are so many guards, it seems impossible to get in."

"No," replied the boy confidently, "it is very simple to get in, if one knows how and where to enter. We do it all the time."

"But with all the soldiers and police, how do you do it?"

"Sometimes we go over the wall at places where there are fewer guards, or those who have little heart to see Jews starved to death. Tonight we will enter through the sewers. You can come along, if you are willing to carry a sack of potatoes on your back."

That chance meeting was Henryk's introduction to Warsaw's famous boy smugglers, who by night dug up potatoes from the fields surrounding the city, then sold them to the ghetto dwellers. Those children were credited with saving or prolonging the lives of many Jewish people during the days before the ghetto was destroyed. Henryk's acquaintance, Peter, was the leader of a band of Polish lads who were, themselves, caught up in the quest for self-preservation.

After darkness had cast a thick blanket over the city, the boys took up their sacks and moved off toward the entrance of the sewer complex that carried away Warsaw's refuse. They crept quietly along the streets, just out of the vision of the men who were about the wearying business of keeping the Jews penned up to die.

As the boys entered the sewer, it was immediately apparent that Peter knew the subterranean passages very well. For Henryk, it was an unpleasant initiation into the smuggling business. Heavy odors from the new environment seemed to immobilize his lungs for a moment. He drew quick, reluctant breaths. The wetness underfoot was heavy with slime, into which his feet sank deeply under the weight of the potatoes. His first impulse was to retreat quickly into the freshness of the night air. He was, however, driven by a desire for reunion that pushed him forward toward his destination.

Finally, the boys and their cargo ascended to street level, and they pushed their way out into the darkness. For a time they sat in the street drawing deep breaths of clean air.

Peter gave orders to his comrades to stay put until he returned. Turning to Henryk, he said, "Follow me and I will show you a place where you can spend the night." He led him to a niche beneath a porch at the rear of one of the buildings. "I sometimes sleep here myself. It will do for shelter until morning; then you can search for your friends. Good luck!" Peter's form melted quickly into the murk as he left to go about his business.

Henryk awakened the next morning to

find a bright sun penetrating the ghetto. Now he would begin to look for his parents. Striding quickly from between buildings, he entered the street. The sights that greeted him were beyond belief. Never had he seen so many people in so small an area. Even at this early hour, people seemed to swarm like flies in the street.

Over one-half million Jews had been forced into the Warsaw ghetto. One hundred fifty thousand of them were refugees who, like Henryk's parents, had been forced to relocate there. They lived everywhere. Schools, deserted buildings, and the streets quartered the gaunt masses.

Starvation and disease were the twin sovereigns of the ghetto. Henryk winched at the sight of emaciated, ragged children with outstretched hands pleading, "I am hungry. Please, give me bread."

Scattered here and there, close to the buildings, were the elderly and the very young, huddled in frail bodies, inching their way toward the end of physical suffering. Some waited silently, while others lifted feeble hands and uttered pitiful entreaties. Now and then he could hear mumbled prayers for the Messiah to come suddenly and bring deliverance.

Scores of those who walked the street bore the ravages of disease on their faces. Estimates reckon that perhaps as many as

150,000 ghetto dwellers in Warsaw were afflicted by typhus. Tuberculosis, dysentery, and a host of related maladies added fuel to their miseries.

Also obvious were the vacant stares of those who had been scarred psychologically to a point beyond recall to the rational world. The suffering and torment had accumulated until all mental sensibilities had been overloaded. Then they exploded, leaving only pathetic physical remnants of once vital people. Those were led about by loved ones, or wandered aimlessly about waiting to be released from their prison.

Henryk stood mesmerized by the variegated smells, sights, and sounds assaulting his senses. Suddenly he became aware of a clattering sound coming slowly up the street. He looked about to see a pushcart attended by two men with handkerchiefs over their faces. Human remains were stacked on the carts like cordwood, as the members of the death crew gathered the bodies of those who had expired during the night. Arms and legs protruded in grotesque gestures, amid expressionless faces that stared openmouthed into the autumn sky. For them, the arduous journey was over. Others, however, would live to see the dying go on.

All that day Henryk walked the streets searching faces of passersby in hopes of finding a familiar figure. Occasionally he paused to inquire about his parents. Some people would shake their heads and walk on without so much as a word. One man stopped to listen patiently to the anxious boy. "I have never heard of such a one," the man said. "Maybe they are all dead like so many of the others."

That answer did not satisfy Henryk. *It can't be*, he thought. *Not all three of them.* That night he retreated to his little haven, discouraged but determined to continue looking until he found them.

It was nearly noon of the following day when he saw a familiar face. It was Mordecai Friedman, a wealthy Jewish man who had lived a few doors from them in the old neighborhood. The old man was turning a corner when Henryk spotted him. Determined to catch the man before he became lost in the press of people, the boy ran after his one-time neighbor. The man stopped as the lad called to him. "Mr. Friedman! Wait! Wait, I must talk to you."

For a moment the old man's brow furrowed. Then his face lit up as he recognized his small pursuer. "Henryk! Henryk Weichert! Can it be you? The last I knew of you, you had been sent off to an orphanage. Now you are here in the ghetto! Come, let us sit down on this step, you must tell me how you have come to be in this place."

The boy and the elderly gentleman sat down together and began to talk of other days. Henryk related his experiences to his friend, who listened with great interest. It was strange that these two, who had barely known each other except by name and face, were now so completely bound together by the thread of the past. It seemed that even recalling the memories of better times was a balm that fleetingly turned minds from their current stresses. When the lad paused, the old man asked about his parents. "Mendel and Ruth, Henryk—are you with them here?"

"No," the boy replied. "I am searching for them. Can you tell me where they are?"

"I am afraid not," was the disappointing reply. "They came here at the same time I did, but I have long since lost track of them."

Henryk asked him if he knew of the address Janusz's father had given him. "Yes, I know the place, and I will tell you how to get there. But you must know that there are now no addresses in this place. Those who lived as one family in a small flat now have ten families living there. It is virtually impossible to find anyone here. If you have good luck, you may run across them. If not, perhaps they are dead.

"Henryk, let me give you some advice before we part. Don't spend too much time

39

looking for them. You are a boy, and still strong. If you stay here in the ghetto, soon you will grow weak like the rest. Don't die here. Do everything you can to save yourself.

"And now my young friend, good-bye. Let us hope the next time we meet will be a better day for both of us." He thrust out a bony hand and patted Henryk's shoulder in a parting gesture, then ambled off down the street.

Henryk knew the old man had given him sound advice. Still, he did not feel he could leave until he was certain there was no hope of finding them.

The address he had been given did not lead him to his parents or provide any further clue as to their whereabouts. Always the answer was the same: "So many have died. Perhaps they are gone too."

After a few more days of searching, with only starvation rations to eat, Henryk began to feel the effects of the lack of food. Friedman's words came back to him. He must not stay here and die. But he did not wish to give up the search either. Upon weighing his options, he decided to leave the ghetto and dig some potatoes for himself. He would then set up a business as a smuggler and sell food to the people in the ghetto. It was a dangerous occupation, but there was no other avenue that logically seemed open to him. He would go over the wall that night and look for food. Henryk had little trouble getting out of the ghetto. He was quick and agile—like a cat on the wall.

In addition to the physical attributes one needed for this hazardous occupation, it was necessary to be possessed by a supreme sense of self-confidence or be driven by sheer desperation. Henryk had a measure of both. He was quite willing to take the chances involved, in the belief that his wits and agility would serve to get him past the guards and back again. Hunger and the conviction that he must live long enough to see his family maintained the fire that provided the mental impetus to go on.

Once he was out of the city, he had but a short distance to go before he came to a small village. Outside the town lay several fields with potatoes enough to serve his purpose. Henryk burrowed along the rows until he had unearthed a sufficient quantity to fill both his stomach and the sack he carried. Slinging the lumpy load over his shoulder, he made for the city in search of a customer for his first transaction. Next morning, it did not take long to find an interested party.

The man was tall and haggard. Several children clustered about him looking hungrily at Henryk's treasure. "Wait just a moment, until I get a box," the man instructed.

Within moments, he returned carrying a small container. As the boy began to transfer the precious potatoes to the box, the man and the childen began knocking them away. No sooner had they hit the ground than the children scooped them up and thrust them into ragged pockets. Few of them reached their intended destination. The man hefted the box and balanced it for a moment. "It looks like you have about eight pounds here," he said.

Henryk was livid with anger. "It is more like twenty," he thundered.

"No, I will pay you for eight pounds of potatoes."

"But I risked my life to bring them to the ghetto. Now you are trying to steal them from me."

The man spoke tersely. "If you don't like it, take them elsewhere."

His impulse to assault the people who were cheating him was almost overwhelming. Then he looked into their faces and the rage drained from him. How could he bring himself to fight against these bags of bones? With a weak nod of the head he held out his hand. The man dropped in a few coins and departed.

Henryk's career as a smuggler was over almost as soon as it had begun. That first encounter soured him on being a ghetto trader. He would wait until nightfall and go over the wall.

While it was still daylight, the boy took a careful survey in order to find the most appropriate place from which to make his escape. The wall was about eight feet high, so it was advantageous to pick a spot where the ground below was relatively soft. Henryk selected a likely looking place, then retreated to await darkness.

A cold rain, which began falling late in the afternoon, was coming down in torrents as he lithely mounted the top of the wall. He perched there for a moment, peering into impenetrable darkness so thick that he could not see the ground below him. He listened intently for a few seconds. Nothing stirred. Fleetingly he thought, *What will be, will be*, and flung his small body into the darkness. Henryk landed with a soggy thud. To his dismay, he had come down squarely between two guards who were standing close to the wall in an effort to keep dry. His sudden descent momentarily startled them into inaction. The boy hit the ground, running as fast as his scrawny legs would carry him. When the flustered guards gained their wits, they began to cry into the rainswept evening: "Halt! Halt at once." Their guns began spitting small darts of flame toward the sounds of the youngster's splashing feet. He could hear the shots and the whine of bullets speeding past him. It was as though the shouts and the bullets had issued a new order for him to hasten his departure. Flying legs seemed to become motorized as he scrambled toward the safety of some bombed-out buildings that stood a short distance from the wall. He managed to reach them before the bullets found him. Diving into the rubble, the young escapee lay listening. Breath came in painful gasps, and his heart raced as though it were completely out of control. A few yards away, he could hear the guards groping through the ruined houses in search of their quarry. He pressed his frail body against the debris and waited. In due time the men gave up the hunt and returned to their posts. With their departure, Henryk was up and running again. When he had gone what he considered a safe distance, he sought shelter and waited for the rain to stop.

Now the question was what to do. He was cold, wet, and hungry. Something must be found to eat. After that, he would seek shelter. The rain had stopped when Henryk stepped out into one of Warsaw's lighted boulevards. Shoppers, delayed because of the rains, were out late. Consequently, quite a number of people were on the street. The hungry youth was eyed suspiciously by a storeowner as he paused to browse in front of his shop. Small baskets of fat, red apples sat displayed beside other fruits and vegetables along the sidewalk.

Henryk made his plans. The money he had received for the potatoes would be of no use to him here. It was currency issued specifically for use in the ghetto. To offer it to anyone outside the wall would be a sure giveaway of his identity. Desperation drove him to a decision. He would wait until the proprietor was distracted, then steal something and make his escape. Henryk wandered slowly to the front of the next shop up the street and feigned interest in the goods displayed in the window. Presently, a woman came to the store and ordered some cherries. As the owner turned away to measure out the purchase, the youngster dashed in to grab up a basket of apples and run up the street. Not far behind, the storeowner charged after him, shouting at the top of his lungs: "Stop thief! Someone stop the thief."

People along the boulevard saw what was happening. But rather than help apprehend the boy, they stood aside and let him pass. They had no stomach for contributing to the prolonged hunger of one of Warsaw's waifs. Soon the man gave up his futile chase. Leaving the lighted area, Henryk searched until he found what appeared to be a short tunnel that ran beneath some of the bombed-out buildings. It was partially filled with rubble but relatively warm. At least it would be a safe place to pass the night.

The small boy sat alone in the dark and munched his apples. *Well,* he thought, *now I am assured of living to see tomorrow.*

The next morning Henryk awakened to a grisly scene that severely strained his youthful powers of manly self-control. Scattered amid the debris choking the tunnel were the skeletons of people who had been killed during the bombing of the city by the Germans in 1939. Henryk had spent the night in the company of the dead. As the horrified child fled from his ghastly companions, it was almost as if something dreadfully symbolic were being projected: For years to come, this lad would be fleeing from the presence of death.

For the next few weeks he would attempt to squeeze out a living by carrying heavy bags for travelers who passed through the Central Train Station. That was not much more rewarding than his first enterprise had been. He and other boys his age were repeatedly chased from the station by police and the adult baggage handlers. Tiring of the kicks and threats of his hide-and-seek existence, he decided to leave the city.

With his future a bleak question mark, Henryk took to the roads away from Warsaw seeking a means to sustain the frail thread of life.

3

The Fuhrer's Herdsman

The countryside around Warsaw was speckled with small farms. A few animals meandered in the fields around ramshackle barns creating a pastoral picture-book effect. Bright winter sun chased the frost from the surface of the dirt roads, causing mud to ooze beneath Henryk's feet as he walked. All in all, it was good to be away from the city. The air was fresh and crisp, there were not so many people, and one saw fewer soldiers. As he tramped along, there was a new feeling about his situation. Perhaps now he could forget some of the things that had befallen him.

Before the day was out, however, his old problems were back again: finding shelter and obtaining food. This, he felt, should not be so difficult here in the country. "I will offer myself to one of the farms to work for them. With so many young men gone to the war, surely there will be a place for me."

Before he made his approach to the first house, Henryk looked himself over. Confessedly, what he saw was somewhat less than impressive. His clothes were dirty and rumpled. It had been days since he had had them off or taken a bath. His stature was not, to be sure, one of his best selling-points. He had always been shorter and smaller of frame than other boys his age. Even his heavy-soled, ankle-high shoes, which always appeared much too large, would not help elevate him appreciably. He had suffered significant weight loss during his recent ordeal, but his winter clothing made him appear to have a little bulk around the middle and in the shoulders.

Carefully tucking in his shirt all the way around, he went over his buttons to see that they were in proper order. Blond hair, which always seemed to have a way of falling back down over his forehead, was raked into place with his fingers. In a last effort to become reasonably presentable, he paused at a stream to dash some cold water on his face. On his way up the walk he made a stab at shaking some of the mud from his shoes. Henryk was ready to apply for a position.

The farmer was heavy-set and did not look too friendly. "What can I do for you?" he asked.

"I am looking for work," the boy replied hopefully.

"You are only a child," the man countered. "You could not do the heavy work on this farm."

"But I can," Henryk fired back. "Yes, I am small, yet I can do any work you ask of me. You will see, I am a good worker."

The man seemed to soften momentarily. "Where are you from?" he questioned.

"I am from Warsaw, but there is no food for me there now."

"Do you have papers?" the farmer queried.

"No, sir."

"Are you a Jew?"

"No, sir, I am not."

The man stood thoughtfully for a moment. Then he began to shake his head slowly. "No—no," he said. "There is too much risk involved. I cannot take the chance. I have no place for you in my house."

As the disappointed youth left the yard, he was murmuring to himself. "Why is it such a terrible thing to be a Jew? Mother was right. No one must ever know who I really am."

During this period people throughout Poland lived in constant fear for their lives. Harboring or being found in the company of a Jew could mean death. Those who collaborated with the Nazis and turned in a person known by them to be Jewish received a reward—bottles of vodka or an increased food ration were among items often used as incentives to this end. To add to the general terror of the people, many who roamed the countryside were notorious thieves or, worse yet, informers who would report their countrymen for the most incidental violations of the rules of the Reich. As a result, Poles had inordinate suspicions about strangers, even very small ones.

Henryk had a marked advantage over most of his Jewish kinsmen. His facial features and coloration did not harmonize with the Jewish stereotype. He had cotton-white hair and bright blue eyes. Furthermore, he did not speak with a pronounced Jewish dialect. That was due in part to his days in the orphanage, which had isolated him completely from other Jews. Those physical and linguistic features allayed suspicions that he might be Jewish, and in so doing contributed to his survival.

All that day he met the same response: "Too small; no papers; sorry, nothing for you here."

Soon an empty stomach began to send its familiar message to his brain. He must look for food. It was, in fact, a simpler and much less hazardous task to obtain sustenance in the country—even if the fare was less than exotic. The fields, where he had once found an abundant supply of potatoes, were now frozen, so he was cut off from that source. As he passed a farmhouse, he saw his staple victual being served by a local farmer. The man was throwing potatoes and peelings into his pigpen. Henryk waited until the farmer returned to the house before moving in to share the meal. Pushing the reluctant hogs aside, he managed to get a fair portion of the food.

Barns, he found, also contained numerous items to be claimed by those who, like himself, were emboldened by hunger. A few days of this kind of foraging would have the color back in his cheeks and the strength flowing to his muscles.

Sleeping presented a problem of another kind. But the thick woods hovering beside the roads offered an adequate solution. One could always find a low place and crawl up under a fallen log. Leaves, which covered the ground with a thick blanket, provided insulation enough to ward off the cold of those early winter months when pulled about a body in sufficient quantity.

Eventually Henryk found his way to the door of a rather large, and by the standards of the times, prosperous farm—large, Henryk would learn, because it actually comprised several farms confiscated from hapless Poles. People were driven from their lands, which were given to loyal Nazis who would manage them for the Fatherland. From the number of livestock in the fields, it appeared that there would be plenty of work to do about the place. An anemic-looking girl answered the knock and quickly retreated to beckon her father.

When the man appeared in the doorway, Henryk was taken aback. For a moment he thought he had come face to face with the Fuhrer himself. The farmer had a square patch of mustache nestled atop his upper lip. His hair was jet black, parted on the right side and swept down, Hitler style, across the left side of the forehead. He was a large man—obviously strong and charged with energy. Henryk noticed that when he talked he had a strange way of twitching the thatch beneath his nose. It appeared he was perpetually attempting to adjust it to a comfortable position.

"Do you have work for me here?" Henryk began.

The look-alike fuhrer eyed the young applicant very carefully. "Yes, there is a great deal of work to do here, but you are just a little one," he said.

"Please, at least give me a chance. I will show you that I can be a good worker," the boy pleaded.

"Well, you are big enough to tend the cows and carry water," the farmer said. "How much do you charge?"

Elated, Henryk responded, "Give me food and a place to sleep. If you think I am a good worker, then you can pay me something."

"All right, you can work here for me. But first I must have a look at your papers."

The lad's heart sank. "I have no papers, they have been lost."

The man's face was stern. "Are you a Jew?"

"No, I am not."

"Are you sure you are not lying to me?"

"No, I am Polish."

"Well then, we will not worry about the papers. I can see to it that you get them."

The boy would soon learn why his new employer was not overly concerned about the lack of proper identification. As his appearance had indicated, the man was a fanatical Nazi. He was also a very influential man in the district. His influence was sufficient to obtain the necessary papers for his young tenant (which he eventually did) with no questions asked. This man was also in desperate need of help. All six of his sons were in the armed forces serving on the Russian front. He was, therefore, left with only his fragile daughter at home.

Henryk was feeling much better. At last he had regular employment and a table at which he could eat—although he was not allowed to eat with the family, but at a small table beside the door in the kitchen.

That made little difference to the famished boy. The food was what mattered.

Sleeping accommodations were spartan by any standard. He would be allowed to sleep in the barn. It was dirty, but the animals' bodies provided heat to keep him warm. After all he had been through, the place seemed like the Grand Palace Hotel.

His position on the farm was to serve as a herdsman to the forty cows owned by the German. Beside the feeding and milking chores, he was charged with keeping an eye out for the interests of his employer. Many hungry people were about the countryside, and the temptation was strong in some of them to indulge in impromptu feasts off quickly slaughtered cows. Others, who had little milk for their children, were given to premature milking sessions at some obscure corner of the pasture. A pair of eyes on the scene throughout the day provided the best deterrent available.

A fringe benefit of Henryk's job was a ready supply of milk for his personal needs. At the table, he was allowed only the residue from milk that had the cream removed. In the barn he had a constant source of fresh whole milk.

The work also gave him the opportunity to meet and establish friendships with Polish people from the neighboring farms. For all of his past difficulties, Henryk remained a very outgoing boy who was constantly on the alert for someone with whom he could converse, particularly those in a position to teach him something. He had learned through bitter necessity to be wary, cunning, and deceptive, but in the process he retained an openhearted warmth people found was easy to respond to.

The German was not aware that his young laborer could understand the language of his mother country. For his part, Henryk was careful not to betray the secret. Consequently, the farmer addressed him only in Polish. Family conversation was always carried on in German. As a result, the lad learned a great deal about the man's activities as a Nazi from the unguarded talk with the wife and daughter at mealtime. The man harbored a deep hatred for the Polish people. He, in the prevailing spirit of National Socialism, saw them as a permanently inferior class of subhumans who deserved to be removed from the face of the earth. He was, in reality, an extremely cruel man who garnered all he could for himself, while giving as little as possible in return. Henryk would feel the lash of that philosophy on more than one occasion.

With the advent of summer, the young herdsman found that his living quarters had been invaded by a new generation of inhabitants—lice were everywhere. Before long, Henryk's body was so thoroughly infested with the tiny creatures that his head became a mass of bleeding sores. When he approached the farmer to ask for ten cents to have his head shaved, the man exploded. "You Polish pig!" he shouted. "Do you dare ask me for money? Get out of my sight before I give you something that will be worse than a few sores on your head."

The boy said nothing. Over the months he had been on the place, he had learned how to hold his tongue while in the presence of his volatile master. Fortunately, he had other hands to help him in time of need. One of the Polish families with whom Henryk had struck up an aquaintance offered immediate assistance to the skinny little fellow. While the husband cut his hair, the woman of the house prepared a kettle of hot water to warm a tub for bathing—a luxury he had not been allowed by the Nazi. While he was in the water scrubbing himself, the man burned his infested clothing and brought him a fresh change from the family supply. It felt good to be rid of the crawling, biting pests that had come to regard him as their personal feeding ground.

Cherished hours were passed with that family. Henryk took great pains to show his appreciation for such acts of kindness. In response to their constant complaints that they did not know what was going on about them—Polish people were forbidden radios and allowed only newspapers printed in German—he confided that he could read German. Thereafter, their private interpreter held regular sessions in their home at which he would read aloud the news from the papers the man picked up in the village.

Another face became welcomely familiar during the days of servitude to the mini-fuhrer. At first it was just a smile and the wave of a hand as the postman passed the road with the mail. But as the months wore on, greetings progressed through stages to long conversations. This mailman was a veritable wellspring of information. He knew all about local personalities and the state of national affairs. Henryk learned a great deal from him that was not to be found in the carefully censored publications allowed them by the Germans. He was particularly fascinated by the tall one's running commentary on the progress of the war, along with editorial comments on the ultimate outcome. It was obvious that the lanky carrier, who had several children of his own, had developed a fondness for the boy who served the gruff taskmaster.

This was a man who had abundant troubles of his own. The police, Henryk learned, had him under surveillance as one who might be engaged in dubious activities. They were, therefore, making it difficult for him to augment his meager income. As a result, he was encountering problems providing for his family. The coarse, black bread available to them was hardly fit for human consumption. Milk was a watery variety akin to what the Nazi put on the table for Henryk. With the approach of winter, fresh vegetables would again be virtually impossible to obtain. The boy's friend was, indeed, a man who could use a helping hand. Henryk decided to launch a one-man relief operation. The situation was not too big for him to handle.

The mailman was surprised, and profusely grateful, when his young confidant ceremoniously offered him some eggs and two bottles of milk.

"But my friend," the postman protested, "I have nothing with which to pay you for these things. And besides, you are placing yourself in great danger by bringing them here to me."

"No," said Henryk, "it is never wrong to steal from a thief. The Germans stole the land from Polish farmers. Then they took the cows and the chickens. None of this belongs to them; it is as much yours and mine as it is theirs. Besides, he will never miss what little I bring to you."

The little fellow did not expect anything in return for what he brought for the family. But one day the postman reached into his bag and brought out a pair of worn but serviceable shoes and handed them to Henryk. On another visit he pressed a coin into his hand. Shortly, an exchange program was in full swing. Before his friend would arrive with the mail, Henryk hurried out to a hollow tree, which had become a prearranged drop place, to fill the larder. After the mailman had passed, he would return to retrieve the small items that were often left in return for his generosity. Trips to the tree became a happy adventure for the youngster. For the months that the exchange was carried on, it provided the central joy in his life.

But it would all come to an abrupt end when the postman approached the house one afternoon with a somber expression on his long face. Henryk was in the lot, bringing the cows into the barn for milking. Catching the boy's eye, he shook his head and turned six fingers toward the ground. The message was clear; all six of the farmer's sons had been killed on the Russian front. The news came to the Nazi only a few days after he had learned of the death of his two brothers in the same war sector. The bad tidings would spell trouble for the child herdsman.

4

That Swine Will Die

News of the deaths sent the farmer into a frenzy. Henryk had, on other occasions, seen him react with unreasoning fury against animals about the farm that had offended him in some small way. He had never, however, seen him quite like this. As he passed the house, he could catch glimpses through the window of the man stalking about the room flailing his arms and ranting in German. The mustached follower of the Fuhrer was completely beside himself.

Henryk hesitated to enter the house for his meal that evening, but he knew that even a slight delay in his arrival might offer an excuse for the man to vent his anguish on him. The boy went in and sat down at his table just inside the kitchen. In the next room, where the family dined, the Nazi ignored his food in favor of a rambling diatribe against the Russians and their allies who were resisting Hitler's brand of deliverance. His wife made one or two feeble suggestions that he calm down and eat his food. But she, too, knew better than to say too much at the wrong time. As he continued, ominous words fell from his mouth — words that sent a quick shiver through Henryk's mind and body.

"The Russian dogs have killed my brothers and my sons," the agitated farmer stormed. "All I have left is a Polish pig. Why should I make a good life for him while my sons lie dead in the snow? Tonight I will fix it. That Polish swine, too, will learn how it feels to die — I will kill him!"

His wife responded to the irrational outburst: "Do what you wish. I have nothing to say."

With the gruesome objective stated, the man calmed down somewhat.

Henryk's first impulse was to flee the house immediately. A quick mental appraisal of his situation counseled otherwise. He must not, at all costs, betray the fact that he understood what the man had said. He must conduct himself as though he suspected nothing. His mind was racing as he finished his meal, rose, and walked to the door of the dining room. Trying to maintain a casual tone, the boy said, "I am going to sleep now. Good night."

"Yes, sleep well," answered the man who intended to kill him. "You have been working hard. Tomorrow I will give you a free day." His voice sounded almost pleasant.

"Thank you very much," the lad replied. He had no intention to stay around and see just what kind of freedom his employer was talking about.

A new snow was falling as he walked the short distance between the house and the barn. He must now act with haste to make preparations for his departure. Realizing that he faced a night in the cold, he pulled on as much clothing as he could. Henryk picked up a sack and put in several of the choice items he had received from the postman. Everything else would have to be left behind, except for some crusts of bread he had spirited from the kitchen. He stood for a moment peering toward the house through a crack between the barn's siding. Seeing no movement, he slipped quietly through the door. Across the barnyard stood the small building where the family's supply of cured meat was kept. He thrust a few pieces into the sack. Before bidding farewell to the place he had called home for over a year, Henryk snatched two roosting chickens from their perch in the henhouse. He was now prepared to begin his dash for freedom.

The road under Henryk's feet was solidly frozen. As he ran through the night, his footfalls raised a rhythmic sound, as the freshly fallen snow was compressed between shoe leather and ice. The melodic cadence seemed to spur him along. During the night he passed through several small villages in his attempt to put as much ground as possible between himself and his would-be persecutor. The man, he knew, was widely known throughout the area. He couldn't risk stopping while there was a chance of being caught and turned over to him. Each time he was tempted to pause for awhile, he could hear the grim words: "The Polish swine will die tonight." No further incentive was necessary. If he slowed to a walk, the cold would soon invade his garments and prompt him to break into a trot again.

As morning neared, exhaustion and the cold forced him toward the doors of homes in a village. He was turned away several times before a woman offered him a bit of warm water and a towel with which he could sponge his dripping features. She refused his request to rest there, however, and he was forced to seek another place of refuge.

Later in the morning he found himself looking into the face of a woman who was asking the inevitable question: "Are you a Jew?"

This time Henryk was prepared. "I am Polish," he replied. He quickly stuck his hand into his pocket and produced the identification papers the farmer had obtained for him.

"All right, you may come in and rest for a few hours; but after that you must leave." The woman's words were music to his frigid ears. She would give him food, but first he must get out of the clothes that were saturated by sweat and melted snow. While he was undressing, she disappeared momentarily. When she returned, she carried suitable replacements from a supply her own boys had outgrown.

After he had warmed up a bit, she sat him down at a table and served tea and hot food. The tired boy savored the meal. It seemed as though the warmth of the tea began to move perceptibly into his fingers and feet. When he had finished, the grateful guest rose from the table and strode to the porch to retrieve his bag. Reaching in, he produced the chickens that had spent the night in close confinement and triumphantly offered them to his hostess. She eyed him suspiciously. "These chickens are not yours," she said sharply. "Where did you steal them?"

Judging from the tone in her voice, Henryk suspected that if he did not come up with a suitable answer, it would mean a sudden return to the hostile environment. He decided to gamble on the truth. He told her about his days with the Nazi farmer, and the succession of events leading to his hasty departure. As the story unfolded, the corners of her mouth began to turn up in a restrained smile. Finally, she interrupted him. "All right. Good, good. To steal from a German or a Jew is acceptable; I will keep your chickens."

She then showed him into a bedroom and told him he could stay there until the next morning. Many months had gone by since Henryk had last slept in a room. It felt strange at first to be in a real bed, devoid of scratchy straw and creeping things. He pulled the covers up to his chin and stretched his tired limbs as far as he could. It was good to be a boy in a house again.

Henryk left the house the next morning refreshed and ready to follow his fortunes. The necessity to remove himself still farther from his former employer was a consideration that must be served, so he continued on a course that took him back briefly to Warsaw. Nothing had changed there, so with only a look at the ghetto from without, he pressed on to other places. For the remainder of the winter he led a vagabond life moving among the villages southeast of Warsaw.

By the time the spring of 1943 threw a green mantle over the Polish landscape, Henryk was thirteen and wise to the ways of the road. He had mastered the subtleties of the art of survival, and moved skillfully about the business of making a way for himself. Warm weather was a welcome change from the bitter months just past. When the fresh green fruit and vegetables began to appear in the fields, he felt that he had a new lease on life.

One bright spring day he was tramping along a road that led to the industrial city of Lodz, a city second only to Warsaw in population. As he walked along, a boy, whom he judged to be about eleven years of age, came alongside and fell in step with him. Henryk had met many such wandering boys during his travels, but the sight of this child flabbergasted him. If someone had taken a pen and written "Jew" across his forehead with indelible ink, his identity would not have been more obvious. His features and general appearance were so markedly Jewish that Henryk was amazed he could have gone any appreciable distance on the roads in daylight without being apprehended.

"Where are you going?" the boy ventured.

"I don't know," Henryk replied. "I'm just going. What about you? Where are you going?"

"I don't know either," he said. "I'm running away from the ghetto."

They were nearing a grove of trees, and Henryk suggested they leave the road and stop there to talk. He was well aware of the calculated risks one ran on the roads in daylight. This boy, he knew, needed some quick basic instruction in how to stay alive. Henryk listened to the boy's story. His name was Saul Blum, and he had lived in the city of Lodz with his family. Life in the ghetto there was intolerable, as it had been for Henryk in Warsaw. Consequently, several youngsters had decided to escape and go to Warsaw in the hope that things there would be better for them. Together they had traveled at night and managed to get safely into the ghetto at Warsaw. Saul soon learned that the only choice open to him in either place was where he would prefer to starve to death. So he had left the others to strike out on his own, heading in the general direction of Lodz but not sure where he should go. With a sympathetic ear to pour his troubles into, the boy talked on and on. Often tears would well up in his eyes as he described the conditions they had been forced to endure and the indignities they suffered at the hands of the Nazis and anti-Semitic Poles. As Saul talked, Henryk looked at him and nearly wept himself. The boy wore all the marks of his agony. Malnutrition had marred his dark features, causing his eyes to appear much too large for his face. His clothing was as ragged as his nervous system. The youth was in a state of complete demoralization, which perhaps explained why he had thrown caution to the winds and exposed himself to such obvious danger.

Henryk draped an arm around Saul's emaciated shoulders. "I understand all about what you have gone through. Now we must find a way to see to it that you can stay alive until the war is over," he said comfortingly.

"Don't say you understand about the ghetto. They don't lock Polish people up so they will die. You cannot possibly understand how terrible the place is," said the boy, who by now was almost shouting.

"But I am not Polish," Henryk confided. "Like you, I am a Jew. My parents and sister were taken to the ghetto in Warsaw. I, myself, have been there. Believe me when I say I know what it is like."

"You are a Jew? It cannot be. To meet another Jew here, it must be a miracle." He was weeping uncontrollably now.

Henryk allowed him to cry while he did some thinking. This was the first time since leaving his home that he had openly admitted to anyone that he was Jewish. Now he had confessed it without a moment's hesitation. He felt an immediate sense of kinship and responsibility for the youth with the tattered nerves—like he would feel, he thought, if he suddenly came upon one of his own brothers. He felt, too, that he had someone else to live for. Henryk was going to do everything in his power to keep the boy alive.

The first order of business was a stern warning. "If you will stay close to me, and do what I tell you, you will be all right. But you must never show that Jewish face in daylight. There are many Germans around here who would enjoy putting you on the end of a bayonet or using you for target practice. To some Polish people you are worth one bottle of vodka, and they will turn you in at the drop of a hat to get it."

The boy listened without returning a word. A spark of hope was beginning to flicker in his eyes. Henryk continued, "For now, you will stay right where you are while I go and look for some food and a place to spend the night." With that understood, he moved off toward a row of houses to seek shelter and a meal. At the first farm he visited, a kindly farmer responded to his request with a gesture toward the barn. "Certainly, you can sleep there. I have plenty of hay inside. It will make you a good soft bed for the night. Wait here at the door and I will get you something to eat." The man returned with bread, milk, and a few potatoes. Henryk thanked him and took them into the barn and left them there. Saul would have a pleasant surprise waiting for him when he came to their lodging place.

Henryk watched in wonder as his companion wolfed down the food he had set before him. It was difficult to believe that a boy this size could consume a meal as ravenously as the eleven-year-old did. When he had finished, Henryk outlined his plans for their future. "We will not travel on the roads in the daylight. When we move, it will be at night so no one will see you. I will seek food and shelter for both of us. Your job will be staying out of sight."

The system worked well. Saul would keep to the woods while his friend foraged. A large grove of fruit trees, supplemented by fresh vegetables gathered at night, supplied their present needs abundantly. Before long the boy, who had been little more than a rack of bones, was fleshing out and in much better spirits. The companionship was beneficial to both of the young wanderers. For Henryk it was good to finally have someone he could talk with openly. The boys spent many hours in satisfying conversation, sharing needs, and pondering questions.

After several weeks of traveling, Saul began to show signs of depression. Henryk attempted to cheer him up, but the boy grew progressively worse. "I want to return to the ghetto at Lodz and be with my parents," Saul said.

"You cannot think of going there," Henryk

objected. "It is too dangerous. There are German soldiers everywhere in Lodz. You will be in great danger of being killed—please, don't do it."

"But my parents live in a house close to the wall. Maybe I can go there in the night and see them from the outside. Perhaps I can get their attention and speak to them."

"Listen to me," Henryk said earnestly. "We cannot act as blind fools. When I left the ghetto, I knew I must take my life in my own hands. If my parents are dead, I cannot help them by dying too. Neither can you. Your life is in your hands, and you must save it. Anyway, if you do succeed in getting into the ghetto, what is there for you then? A quick death at the hands of the Germans is better than slow starvation in the ghetto. If you want to die, go to a German and say, 'Look, I am a Jew. Take me and shoot me in the head.'"

The impassioned speech fell on deaf ears. Saul had already decided what course he would take. To attempt to dissuade him any longer was futile. Henryk gave in. "If you must go, I will go with you as far as the outskirts of the city. Then you will be on your own."

The journey to Lodz was uneventful, until they came to a village close to the city. "I want to stop here," Saul told Henryk. "My relatives lived here before they were taken to the ghetto. I spent much time with them and came to know this place very well. There is a market here where the owner keeps his money in the open in a box. I will go there and take some money to give to my parents when I see them."

Again Henryk warned him of the possible danger of being caught. Saul assured him, "I will not be in danger. The owner is old and fat. I will have no trouble getting away from him."

Henryk had reservations, but Saul gave him no choice in the matter. The boys entered the village just as dusk was falling. Saul led them straight to the market, which was located near the center of the town. The establishment had a covered roof but was open on both sides, making access from either street possible. They stopped on the corner in front of the market. Henryk watched as Saul entered the shop and made straight for the cash box. Without hesitating he thrust in his hand and came up with a fistful of money. Before the startled store owner could react, he ran to the other side of the market and out into the street. His friend was horrified as he realized that the boy was running squarely into the arms of a German policeman who was coming up the street. The youth, who was driven by homesickness and a compulsion to help his parents, had no chance at all. The policeman got a firm grip on the boy as a patroling German soldier rushed to the scene. The man looked at Saul's face and cursed loudly. "This little thief is a Jew!" he called to the approaching soldier.

"We know what to do with Jew pigs," the soldier called back.

Henryk felt nauseated as he saw the soldier reach out to take the boy by the throat and lift him to eye level. The coins tumbled from his hand as his eyes rolled wildly and his tongue was forced from his mouth by the strangling grip of the soldier's hand. As Henryk turned to leave the scene, the soldier was dragging the boy backward up the street.

For days afterward, Henryk bore the weight of severe depression. Saul had been more than a friend to him. In a sense, he had represented the hope that if they could help each other survive until the war was over, they would, each through the other, have a link to the future. There would be someone else who had suffered with him and survived—someone who knew how it really was.

The young man who had accumulated so many mental and physical scars would take on yet two more: an enduring memory of the sound of coins striking the pavement, and the mental picture of the distorted face of his young friend. Henryk sat alone and lonely, wondering about it all. To live, to die — it all seemed so futile. Maybe the dead were better off than those who were unfortunate enough to continue to exist. Why did he even care to go on? What purpose could possibly be in it? Sleep extinguished the fire of frustration that raged in his emotions.

5

All In a Day's Work

Like a hunted rabbit returning to its lair, Henryk was drawn repeatedly back to Warsaw. The magnetism created by the slim possibility that his parents were still alive was irresistible. His experience with Saul rekindled the desire to find some trace of his family's whereabouts. His arrival in Warsaw in the early days of May, 1943, brought him on the scene in time to witness the death thrones of the ghetto. Flames from the giant funeral pyre leaped toward the sky as entire blocks of buildings were systematically destroyed.

By mid-July, 1942, Heinrich Himmler, who was in charge of implementing Hitler's Final Solution, decided that the tenacious Jews in Warsaw were not starving to death fast enough to suit his timetable. Consequently, he issued a directive ordering the massive "resettlement" of ghetto Jews. By year's end, approximately 310,000 Jewish people had been "resettled" in the gas chambers at Treblinka, in preparation for "processing" their remains into fertilizer, soap, hair mattresses, and other ghoulish products created by the Third Reich masterminds. Only 60,000 remained in the ghetto at the beginning of 1943.

In January of the new year, Himmler himself paid a visit to Warsaw and found the presence of so many stubborn Jews eluding his efforts intolerable. S.S. Brigadefuhrer Juergen Stroop was commanded to destroy the ghetto and remove the recalcitrant resisters. General Stroop was a man who fervently shared Adolph Hitler's estimate of Jewry. To him they were "trash and subhumanity." He needed little encouragement to warm to the task before him.

The Jews who remained in the ghetto had come to their own decision: They would issue a declaration of war on their tormentors and go to their graves fighting. One ghetto leader called it "the most hopeless declaration of war ever made." Their assessment of the situation was succinctly summarized in the words of another who observed, "One way or another, lies death."

Originally, the ghetto had covered an area approximately two-and-one-half miles long by one mile wide. Following the major deportations, it was reduced to measure one thousand yards. Beneath the streets, Jews had created a honeycombed concentration of fortifications from which their military operations would be directed. Their weapons were a pitifully meager assortment of pistols, rifles, and a few machine guns which had been smuggled in. The arsenal also contained a supply of homemade molotov cocktails (fire bombs).

Stroop launched his attack against the determined handful of defenders with two thousand troops. They entered the battle armed with all the tools of war available to a modern army: automatic weapons, flamethrowers, howitzers, anti-aircraft artillery, and tanks. He was shocked and infuriated when the ghetto dwellers mounted a defensive action that would frustrate the German force for weeks. The general settled on burning the ghetto one block at a time as the most effective means of terminating the battle. Slowly the invaders began to flush the Jews from their defensive positions. Many Jewish fighters refused to surrender. Some men and women were seen leaping from burning buildings, then dragging their broken bodies into other places of shelter to keep up the fight. Stroop was dumbfounded at the sight of wounded Jews staggering into the flames rather than fall into his hands. Toward the end of the fighting, a group of trapped defenders resorted to a Masada-like mass suicide to avoid being captured.

In the end, of course, the outgunned and overmatched heroes and heroines would be overcome. But they had raised the voice of their pent-up defiance for all the world to hear and remember. For a significant number of them, it was not the end. They disappeared into the sewers to slip past the German dragnet and join the partisans who operated against the common foe. They would continue to fight.

Henryk and the citizens of Warsaw witnessed the tragic drama and stood with faces illuminated by the spectacular fires of the Holocaust. A resounding explosion ended the episode. As a last symbolic act of their triumph, Stroop's soldiers dynamited the Warsaw synagogue. The ghetto no longer existed.

For Henryk, it was one more bitter potion to down. Once again, he turned his back on the city of his childhood. Crossing the Vistula River, he turned north in search of a haven. As if some unseen hand of mercy were moving in to the buffeted child, a door of friendship was readily opened to him. In a village not far from Warsaw proper, he encountered a Polish family who seemed more concerned about the possibility of his being German than fearing that he might be a Jew. A quick look at his identification papers reassured them and they took him in. The father of the family was a rather elderly man who had married late in life. His wife was much younger than he, but she suffered from a debilitating disease. The couple had two strapping sons, Stanislov and Janek, who were eighteen and twenty-three years of age respectively.

In this household, Henryk was not treated as a servant. Here he was taken in as a full member of the family. He occupied a room with a bed of his own. Often the woman would place additional food before him and admonish him to eat well, so he could become big and strong like Stanislov and Janek. The boy eagerly shared the duties around the house and made every contribution that opportunity afforded. The months he spent with the family were indeed a healing time for young Henryk. For the remainder of the year and well into the next, he enjoyed a happy and refreshing interlude.

Trouble, however, was a constant stalker of Jew and Pole alike during those days, and sooner or later it was bound to step through the door. It entered on a morning when Henryk came downstairs to find that the boys were not at home. His inquiry about where they had gone brought only a vague reference to their being at work somewhere. They had, in fact, fled because word came to them that a German sweep of the area would be made to impress all able-bodied males to work on a military installation being constructed nearby. When soldiers came to the house looking for the sons, the father said they had gone to another village to work and he did not know when they would return. When Henryk returned to the house from his hiding place, he found the man badly beaten. He had not revealed the whereabouts of the boys.

Military movements through the villages accelerated. The Russians were making life hard for the Germans, and the ultimate outcome of the conflict was now beginning to be clarified. A number of partisan terrorist groups of varied political persuasions were pressing their clandestine operations in the area. For their part, the Nazis were showing, if such were possible, ever more vicious tendencies. The Ukranians attempted to outdo their German counterparts in deliberate acts of senseless cruelty. Their allegiance to Russia had been thrown over in favor of the Germans earlier in the war. Now they were fully aware of the fate that awaited them if they fell into the hands of their unforgiving former comrades. It was said of the Ukranians, "If it has eyes, they will shoot it." Rape, pillage, and murder were all their specialties. Their wave of terror spread in an ever widening circle throughout the countryside.

It was a sunny day in the early summer of

1944 when a knock came on the door. A man entered the house at the invitation of Henryk's host. He had never seen the visitor before, but it was immediately obvious that the two men were well acquainted. They went into the kitchen and spent some time in conversation before the stranger returned to the room where Henryk was sitting. The boy was impressed with the man's bearing and appearance. He was well dressed, blond, about forty years old. When he spoke, it was apparent that he was well educated. Henryk thought he may have been a doctor or a teacher. He spoke very precise Polish. Without introducing himself, he asked Henryk a question: "What do you think about the Germans?"

The boy was in a dilemma as to what to answer. However he chose to reply, it could mean trouble. He threw any attempt at subterfuge to the winds, and answered forthrightly. "I can tell you plainly that I do not like the Germans," he said emphatically.

"Why not?" the man asked.

"As you can see, I am here alone. As far as I know, all the members of my family are dead. The Germans are responsible for it. That is reason enough for me to be against them. Maybe you are a German—I don't know. But I cannot speak otherwise."

The man smiled. "I can assure you that I am anything but a German, and I am happy to know that we share the same opinion of our enemy." The man talked on for nearly an hour, probing the boy's mind with subtle questions. Finally he got to the point. "How would you like to have a good job?"

"I will do what I can for you. But first I must ask the man I live with if it is all right for me to work for you."

"Never mind about that; it will be acceptable to him," the man answered confidently.

Henryk was not convinced until he had gone to the kitchen and asked his benefactor. "It is fine," he was told. "This man is a member of my family. Do what he asks you.". Thus assured, he returned to the man for instructions.

"About four miles up the road is a town. Just on the other side, on the right, a unit of Hermann Goering's air command is stationed. All the telephone wires running to the headquarters are strung on poles along the road. I want you to go there and cut them. There are many of them. Be sure you cut them all. When you have finished, leave the place as fast as you can. Be very careful. If you are caught, do not tell them where you have come from. Just forget that you came from here. Do not tell them anything."

Henryk set out, as he was told to do, the next afternoon. It was late in the day when he reached his destination. The wires were strung on low poles located close to the road. He selected a spot with some trees clustered about and quickly scaled the pole. The wires made a curious singing noise as he clipped them, and they snapped away to fall to the ground. When he had finished the job and started to descend, he looked down to find himself staring into the menacing gaze of a German soldier who had a rifle leveled at him. The soldier had acid in his voice as he issued his order: "Come down from there, you Polish pig. You are committing sabotage. Don't try anything or I will finish you on the spot."

Henryk hung to the side of the pole for a moment. He did not want to come down, but there was no other alternative left open to him. His career as a partisan, he thought, had come to a disastrous conclusion. The boy was certain he would be shot on the spot. The only small comfort that crossed his mind was in being shot instead of stabbed—a method of being dispatched he had always feared. At least it would, he reckoned, be quick. The soldier, however, had another plan. "Put your hands on your head and walk toward the building beyond the wall." Henryk did as he was commanded and was marched off at bayonet point to the interrogation officer. The young saboteur was shoved rudely into the room where two officers and a sergeant were seated.

"What have we here?" one of the officers inquired.

"He is a small partisan," said the soldier. "I found him cutting telephone wires outside the camp."

An impeccably dressed officer, wearing a monocle, took over the questioning.

"Do you speak German?" he asked.

Henryk did not respond to the question. They concluded that he did not understand German and sent for a Polish interpreter. When they found he could speak Polish, they began.

"Please, sit down," the officer said in a voice that dripped with kindness. "Would you like to have a piece of chocolate?" The boy accepted it and nibbled some half-heartedly.

"Tell me first who it was that sent you here."

"No one."

"How did you come?"

"By myself."

"Who gave you the wire cutters?"

"I found them."

The officer turned to his comrade and spoke in German. "Here is a smart one. We will have to soften him up a bit." He addressed the interpreter next. "Tell him if he tells us the truth, we will allow him to go."

Henryk was not impressed. He knew if he told them what they wanted to know, it would be the last stop on the road for him. They waited a few moments for the offer to sink in, then started at the beginning again. "Now tell us the truth," the man said softly, "who sent you here?"

"This was sport for me," the boy answered. "I like adventure. There was nothing to do and I saw the wires, so I cut them. That's all there was to it."

The German began to tap a pencil on the desk impatiently. Turning slightly, he nodded to the sergeant. The man left the room and came back carrying a short, heavy club. Without a word he raised it quickly and struck the youth a brutal blow across the back. A searing shaft of pain tore through his body, as white blotches danced before his eyes. "Now tell us," shouted the officer.

Henryk registered a negative response.

The sergeant was upon him immediately, bludgeoning him about the head, shoulders, and back. Henryk began to feel his consciousness slipping away as he sank to the floor. A strange wave of serenity passed over him. He felt as though he did not have a care in the world—nothing hurt anymore. Buckets of cold water brought the pain coursing back into his brain. When he had regained consciousness, he was questioned again.

His head had been split open to the bone. Large knots were beginning to come up on his body. In spite of the agony, he was determined to hold his tongue. He felt he was going to be killed whether he gave them the information or not. He knew he could not survive much more beating. Convinced that they would soon finish matters for him, he doggedly shook his head and refused to reveal any information. The beating began all over again. Suddenly it stopped. Through the fog, he could hear the officer ordering the sergeant in German to throw some more water on him.

"We will let him go and have him followed. He will probably lead us to where he came from. If he does not, have the man assigned to follow him kill him. Don't bother to have him brought back here."

He then addressed Henryk through the interpreter. "We have nothing further to say to you. You are free to go."

The bloodied youth managed to pull his battered body slowly out the door and onto the road. He knew he was being followed, but he made no movement that would betray this knowledge to his pursuer. He was just entering the village near the headquarters when he was met by an aged woman, who dropped a basket she was carrying and ran forward at the sight of him. She must have been in her seventies, but she moved like someone much younger. "What has happened to you, child?" she cried, and began wiping the blood from his head with a handkerchief. As she bent over him, the soldier who was following came along, grabbed her roughly by the shoulder, and began to push her away.

"You filthy beast," the enraged woman screamed at him. "Leave this boy alone. I am old; you can kill me if you want someone to murder. But you will not hurt him anymore."

They were struggling with each other when Henryk saw his opportunity to escape. As though he were suddenly charged with some superhuman burst of strength, he ran between some houses and off toward the woods behind the town. Before the German could disengage himself from the elderly protector of children and give chase, Henryk was sprinting into the forest. He ran in large circles until he was on the verge of exhaustion, before falling down to rest and await darkness to provide cover for his trip back home.

When he reached the house, he found it unlocked. The man and woman were not there. He crept inside and went straight to his bed. Now waves of pain raked his body. If he died now, at least it would be in a bed like a human being, not like a dog in a field. About three hours after Henryk returned to the house, the door on the bedroom was pushed slowly open. He waited apprehensively to see who was behind the hand that moved the door. A sense of relief came over him as he saw a middle-aged woman enter the room and come to the bedside. She was a nurse who had been sent by partisans. They had been outside watching for him to return. When they were sure he had not been followed, she was sent in to tend his wounds. The woman examined him and told him to rest until she returned. A short time later she brought a doctor to the house to apply dressings and give him injections for pain.

The next day a man came to him to talk about the mission. He marveled that he had been released by the Germans. The man was convinced about the boy's truthfulness by his condition. He was well aware of the tactics used by the Nazis and knew that had the boy given them information, he would not have been there in any condition.

After several days, the blond gentleman who had sent him to cut the wires paid a call. The partisan leader extended his hand along with his congratulations. "You are a very courageous young man," he said. "You did an important job for us and we are grateful. You rest here until you are well. All your needs will be properly looked after. We will not forget what you have done." The man's word was good. Henryk would spend the next two weeks in bed recovering from the beating. Each day the doctor and nurse would come by to care for him. In addition to the medical attention, they brought along special foods which would supply better nourishment for him. He was overwhelmed by their kindness and genuine concern for his welfare. It was something he had not seen much of over the past five years.

6

In the Presence
Of My Enemies

Henryk's pleasant respite was to be short-lived. Within weeks a new contingent of Ukranians moved into the village and began at once to vent their sadistic malevolence on the villagers. Young men were commandeered for slave labor or shot at the slightest provocation. Henryk decided it was time, once more, to seek refuge in a more favorable place. He bid a fond farewell to the couple who had befriended him for so many months and headed for the bridge across the Vistula. Great changes were about to take place in Warsaw. The Polish were preparing a military uprising against the Germans. Conditions in the capital were abysmally difficult.

The boy found food more difficult to obtain than ever before. Everywhere he went, he was roughly turned aside. His former troubles seemed insignificant when compared to those assailing him now. Those who had a few morsels of food guarded it with their lives. Regardless of how much sentiment they might feel toward the needy, people simply could not risk their own future by giving anything away. It was a day when "every man for himself" was the watchword of life. Henryk's situation was mired in those bleak circumstances when an opportunity sauntered into his path from a totally unexpected source. As he idled along a Warsaw street one morning, a mounted German soldier rode past him toward a corner of the street. Henryk reached the intersection as the man dismounted from the animal he was riding. "You there," he called in the youth's direction. "Come over here." The young man was wary but felt he had best obey the order. "Watch my horse while I go into that shop for a few minutes." Without waiting for an answer he placed the reins in the boy's hands and stepped into the shop. Inspiration is often born by the convergence of necessity and opportunity. In this case, temptation and surrender struck in the same bolt of inspiration. In a flash, the young rustler leaped astride the surprised animal's back, and with a sharp clatter of hoof beats made off down the street. Pistol shots rang out from somewhere behind him, but at the rate he was putting distance between himself and the policeman, there was little chance of his being hit. Henryk pressed the winded steed beyond the city limits and slowed him to a walk when they were a safe distance into the country. The boy was aware of the bargaining power resting beneath the saddle he was seated upon.

The farmer slowly circled the horse several times. He obviously knew it had been commandeered, but he had little present interest in the finer points of the law. Possession was what counted at the moment. Also, he and his countrymen were sure that the German occupation was coming to a close. Consequently, they regarded anything taken from the invaders as a legitimate prize of war.

"What will you take for him?" asked the interested farmer.

"One pig—not too big," answered the young businessman.

"Is that all?" gasped the startled buyer.

"That's all," replied the hungry youth.

The man turned toward the barn. "Come along and pick one out."

Henryk selected a plump young pig and hoisted the struggling animal to his shoulders. As the farmer led the horse to his barn, Henryk and his merchandise took the road back to Warsaw.

Offers for the prize pig came thick and

fast from the hungry citizenry. He succumbed when the price reached 10,000 Zlotys. At that point, boy and pig parted company. A plan had already been well thought out in the boy's mind. He had passed a hotel on many occasions and paused to watch people eat full-course meals over immaculate white tablecloths. Now that he was a man of some means, he would join, at least for one night, the company of the well-to-do. He went into the establishment and carefully selected a table by a window. After he had eaten his fill, he rented a room for the night, took a hot bath, and tumbled into a clean bed for long hours of unbroken sleep. Next morning, after enjoying a good breakfast from what remained of his funds, he left the hotel to begin wandering again.

The Polish uprising against the Germans began on August 1, 1944. Orders for the action came from the Polish government in exile in London. Polish leaders were aware of the fact that the Russian vanguard was approaching the city rapidly, and were determined to attempt to take Warsaw before the Russians could arrive and lay claim to the victory. Even as the battle was being waged between Pole and Hun, tanks from the Russian advance units were being positioned along the opposite banks of the Vistula to watch the slaughter. Joseph Stalin, the Russian dictator, had everything to gain by biding his time—both combatants were considered to be his enemies. Therefore, the more thoroughly they decimated one another, the easier it would be for his forces a few months hence, when they entered the capital city.

The battle would rage through the months of August and September. Initially, the Polish seized half of the city. Their successes were soon negated, however, as the weight of superior German fire power forced them to relinquish their gains. In the course of the conflict, nine-tenths of Warsaw was destroyed. Civilians by the thousands were made refugees, as the city became little more than an armed garrison for German troops.

Conditions for Henryk now reached their lowest ebb. People flooded the villages, and the Germans, who had been forced back across the river by the Russians, were seizing every edible commodity within their grasp. Even the most seasoned foragers were hard pressed to find enough to keep them alive. Henryk sized up the situation and settled on a daring approach to the problem. A detachment of the German Wehrmacht was stationed just outside Warsaw. He would move into the camp of the enemy in quest of a small portion to stave off the persistent hand of hunger.

His estimate of the German oppressor

had not changed. His body still bore vivid reminders of the Nazis' capacity for brutality. The struggle for survival, however, had been reduced to its lowest conceivable denominator. One must seek a source of supply from any quarter available. Pride, ideology, or humanitarian allegiances were immaterial—it was a matter of life or death, food or starvation.

He positioned himself ouside the camp and began offering his services to the officers in exchange for a place at the table. After a number of degrading rebukes, he confronted a colonel who had alighted from the sidecar of a motorcycle. As the mud-spattered officer strode toward the gate, Henryk ran alongside, delivering a verbal list of his credentials. He had run through sweeping, kitchen duty, and bedmaking without much interest being registered by his subject. Then he struck pay dirt. "And I can make those boots shine like they were new." That drew the officer up short.

"Let me see your papers," he said. Looking at them for a moment, he made a sweeping gesture with his head. "You have convinced me, little one. Follow me and I'll give you a chance to show what you can do." Henryk, the gentleman's gentleman, followed close behind his new master as they passed by the guardpost and through the gate. A gruff word from the officer sent a private, who had charged out to challenge Henryk, scurrying back to his position.

The boy was soon occupied with a full round of duties about the camp. Bedmaking, sweeping barracks, and shining officers' boots were all routine responsibilities for him. Kitchen duty was the most productive area in his small sphere of activity. It not only provided for his own needs, but also gave him the opportunity to put aside boxes of scraps from the mess tables to give to Polish civilians who served the Germans in another capacity.

This detachment of troops had, as a part of their duties, the oversight of the looting of the city of Warsaw. The Polish civilians were forced to comb the ruins and ferret out gold, silver, and other valuables people had concealed before their hasty forced departures. All finds were brought to the camp each evening for classification and transport to Germany. The penalty for the retention of even the smallest item by a civilian was being shot on the spot.

Henryk was an instant celebrity among the Polish workers. After his duties for the day were completed, he would bring his box of leftovers to the hungry Poles, who would congregate to pull and shove for a handful of the precious cargo. He even took pains, often at his own risk, to bring them things he picked up around the barracks. The most sought-after commodity was the cigarettes he supplied. All the butts he swept from the floor were kept for redistribution among the workers who were bound by the habit. His horizons were broadened considerably when the Germans asked him to go to a neighboring village and bring back bottles of vodka for them. He explained to the soldiers that he hesitated to attempt to pass the checkpoints for fear he would be taken into custody. The commanding officer remedied the situation by issuing a pass that allowed him to have the run of the area. That freedom afforded a valuable opportunity to do personal reconnaissance, whereby he could keep abreast of troop movements and the preparations by the Russians to move against them. The appreciative Germans gave him money at what amounted to a thirty percent markup on what they had given him to make the purchases. He was soon operating as a young capitalist, and doing a brisk business. The money was used to purchase small items from the post commissary for personal needs and supplies for his Polish friends among the civilians.

One day, as he was making his trip, he stopped to pass some time with a work detail that was busy sifting the debris from ruined shops in a business area. Henryk began idly rummaging through some wreckage in the corner of a shop when his eye fell on a dirty jar that was half filled with small stones. "Worthless glass," called one of the Poles to him. "Throw it away and get out of here before you injure yourself." The boy did as he was told, only to see the man come over and retrieve the container himself. He would learn later that he had cast aside a small fortune in unset diamonds.

Henryk's arrangement with the German soldiers endured for about four months. Gradually Henryk sensed, through his own observation and the air of apprehension obvious among the Germans, that the Russians were beginning to make their move across the river to attack Warsaw. The youth knew that the time was ripe for him to make another flight for self-preservation. He was delicately balanced between the jaws of a great steel trap. Death could come swiftly from German or Russian, depending on whose gunsight framed him first. He would do his best to make it difficult for either to accomplish the final act. His path of flight led him to a town southwest of Warsaw, Grodzish Mazowieki. It was a sizeable community, where Henryk found people who would trade small rations of bread for many hours of labor.

Airstrikes by Russian planes had destroyed some of the buildings in the town. Henryk found one in which the floor had not

collapsed, and he took up residence in the
cellar. He converted the area used for stor-
age of firewood and foodstuffs into a small
apartment, complete with a bed and shelv-
ing for his small cache of food. With the
passage of each new day, the Russian attacks intensified. Within a matter of days
the town was reduced to a gutted graveyard
of burned out buildings. The boy roamed
the streets between attacks, snatching what
he could salvage from burning buildings to
add to his hoard of food.

In mid-January retreating columns of the
broken remnants of the German army,
which had opposed the Russians in Warsaw, swept through Grodzish. Not far behind were the Russians in hot pursuit of
their fleeing adversaries. Shortly afterward, a Russian occupation unit arrived in
the town to secure it and maintain order. As
the thunder of the guns and the drone of
planes passing overhead subsided, Henryk's tired mind slowly assimilated the fact
that for him the long war in Europe had
ended. The tyrant had been banished from
the land—liberation was a reality.

That night, he sat in his shelter and
looked back over the last five years of his
life. Henryk had, he thought, just cause to
congratulate himself. Under the most ad-
verse conditions anyone could possibly endure, he had survived. It was a triumph for

determination, toughness, skill, and a lightening-quick mind over the instruments of intimidation, privation, and death that had been turned against him. Thousands had died, but he had prevailed. In his mind, the garland of victory rested firmly on his head when he laid down to sleep that night.

It was sometime during the next day that he began to realize it was no longer a capital crime to be a Jew. The bone-weary remnant who had concealed identities, hidden in the woods, or occupied lines that had not yet filed into the gas chambers, began to drift to the surface. Identifying armbands and patches with their yellow stars of David could be cast aside—forever, Jews fervently hoped. Now they could begin their efforts at attempting to fit some of the shattered pieces of their lives back together. What Henryk and his fellow Jews found when they emerged from the Holocaust was incomprehensible. Poland's Jewish community had been reduced to an emaciated fragment. Here and there, one or two members out of entire families were still alive. The vast majority of their fellows were not so fortunate—they had passed off the scene, never to be heard from again.

When conditions permitted, Henryk went back to Warsaw and picked his way through the ruins until he found himself on the street that had once been home to him. Some familiar faces, aged almost beyond recognition, were silently moving away the rubble in preparation for a new beginning. The boy sat down on some stones that had been a part of his home. With his past preoccupation with survival no longer a factor, there was an immense void within him—he was alone. Had, by some miracle, any of his family survived? He would spend months trying to find the answer to that question. But for the days that lay immediately before him, until he could begin his search in earnest, he would be engulfed in a consuming agony of loneliness.

7

The Search

People were crowding into the international office of the Red Cross that had been opened in Warsaw. World War II was now in the history books, and Jews were free to press the search for friends and families across the entire face of Europe. When Henryk arrived at the office, he was greeted by two surprises. First, he did not expect to find so many Jewish people there. Living as he had, in almost total isolation, instilled a subconscious feeling that he was completely alone as a survivor. It was difficult to shake off that sensation. The second surprise was equally pleasant. Here and there in the crowd, he saw faces he had known during the days of his childhood. They had changed substantially, but still the tie with the past was revived, and that gave him a sense of being back among the living once more.

He was excited to find an old friend and classmate, Vwadik Jalonka, among those who waited at the center. The young men shared a warm reunion, complete with updates on events which had touched their lives during the war. They parted with a promise to maintain their contacts in the future.

For a time he was distracted from his central purpose. The meeting with Vwadik and observing the emotional reunions taking place between old friends captivated his attention. He was fascinated to see the expressions on the faces of people greeting one another for the first time in tortured years. The way they clung to each other, physically and emotionally, was a sight that nearly overwhelmed the teenage observer. Those people had little else to which they could cling in those early postwar days. Dispossessed from homes and businesses, they had come from behind the barbed wire enclosures. Each carried his own disquieting memories of the nightmare experience. Many bore bright blue identification numbers tattooed on their forearms. Others had left the ranks of the partisans and the wild-animallike existence of the perpetually hunted. Some came to the office with years of living with forged documents behind them. Those people had lived in the Gentile community, where they were seized with constant fear that rose with every knock on the door or walk down the street.

Often they had been forced to submit to extortion imposed on them by people who knew their true identities and found it more profitable to bleed them than to turn them in.

By and large, they all, in one way or another, found that life was still a grim question mark. Most had been refused access to the properties they had owned before the war—those who presently occupied them simply refused to relinquish possession to Jewish people. The Jews, who had been disenfranchised by the coming of the Nazis, found themselves to be displaced people after the Nazis' departure. This somber fact confronted the ravaged survivors: aggressive anti-Semitism was far from dead in Eastern Europe. Hundreds who filed into the Red Cross office had already felt the cruel lash of hatred for Jews that persisted in Poland after the war. Some of those same people would perhaps be among the victims slain in an incomprehensible pogrom that occurred in 1946 in the town of Kielce; Polish citizens formed a mob and brutally murdered forty people, all of whom were survivors of the Holocaust.

In spite of it all, they still had one another. And understandably they held fervently to fellow Jews. They were not a people bound together by lands, social status, or monetary expediencies. They were, every last one of them, dispossessed Jews who had only other Jews with whom to identify. Thus, in a consuming sense, Henryk and all European Jewry would, for the immediate future, be obsessed with the search for survivors.

The woman behind the desk had a kind face that radiated desire to help. Henryk had waited the day out to speak to her. "What can I do for you, child?" the Red Cross representative asked.

"They told me that you might have information about my family."

"If you will give me their names, I will check the list and see if they have been registered at this office."

She wrote as Henryk spoke. "Weichert is the family name. My parents are Mendel and Ruth. They were sent to the ghetto with my sister Tema. I have three brothers, Arthur, Hersh, and Jacob. They were taken to Germany to work."

The woman turned to consult the long list of names that had been turned in. She looked at Henryk and reluctantly informed him, "There are none by this name listed here. But do not be discouraged; we receive hundreds of names every day. Perhaps soon the names of the members of your family will be among them. Come back here tomorrow and listen to the names that are read over the loudspeaker. All new names that come in are read over it during the day."

The boy left the office determined to be there before it opened in the morning so he would not miss hearing the names of those who had joined the list of persons located by the Red Cross.

All through the following day he listened intently to the announcements. The crackle of the loudspeaker had a strange effect on the people who were seated in the office and outside on the street. An immediate hush would fall over them, and all ears would quickly jockey for the best vantage point for hearing the names. Occasionally people would burst into tears or shouts of joy as the name of a family member or close friend came over the speaker. The response had a contagious effect as others in the room would spontaneously join in the jubilation. It seemed at times that they were sharing in a subdued tribute to a monumental triumph—another of their kinsmen had emerged from the sea of suffering and death. For Henryk there would be no tears or shouts of joy. He listened eagerly to each new listing of names. A few were names that he recognized. None, however, were those of the members of his family.

He haunted the central office in Warsaw for many days without satisfaction. Finally, he approached the desk of the woman to whom he had first spoken. "May I see for myself the list of names you have have?" he asked politely.

"Certainly you may," replied the understanding woman. She watched as Henryk ran a stubby finger down the list—lips silently forming the names he saw on the paper. Hesitantly he looked up and slowly slid the worn sheaf of papers across the desk.

"Are there other places where I can look for them?" he questioned.

"Yes, a large center has been opened in the city of Lodz. If you go there, perhaps they can be of some assistance." She looked at him earnestly until she had fully caught his eyes. "And, young man, I do hope you locate them."

Before he left the office he handed her the address of a Polish family he was acquainted with in Warsaw with instructions to inform them if news of his family's whereabouts came in.

Early the next morning he began his journey to the city of Lodz. The residual effects of exposure, bad diet, and the beating he had received at the hands of the Nazis caught up with him there. Henryk found that the center in Lodz had extensive listings of the names of people who had been released from the death camps. He and the desk worker were poring over one of the lists when he began to feel an unsteady sensation in his legs. "Do you feel all right?" the young man who was assisting him asked solicitously.

"No, I feel very weak in my legs, like I am going to fall."

"Sit here. I'll call a doctor."

"We had better move you over to the hospital and have a good look at you," the doctor concluded. Henryk made no effort to protest the decision. It was apparent to him that he needed medical attention.

A Polish physician was in the middle of his examination of the youth when he called a Russian doctor to the bedside. "Come over here. I want you to have a look at this." Then he asked Henryk: "Where did you get all these scars and marks on your body?" Henryk told them they were souvenirs he had received from the Germans. "Well," the doctor replied, "they are souvenirs you will have with you for the remainder of your life." The men were astonished that he had not sustained broken bones from such severe punishment. When they concluded their examination, they prescribed a month's stay in the hospital for rest and recuperation. Henryk would again have an opportunity to taste some of the sweet fruits of compassion he had been denied under the Nazis. As he settled into his hospital bed, he reflected on the fact that in this place the people knew he was a Jew, but it didn't seem to make any difference. He was treated as well as any other patient.

He left the hospital with a feeling of fresh mental and physical vitality. The search, he determined, would continue until he found some trace of his family or became fully convinced they had perished.

Hundreds of new names had been placed on the roll by the time he returned to the Red Cross office in Lodz. It offered no more favorable information for him. He decided to wait there for a few more days and then move on to other centers. After three days of impatiently listening to the names that were coming into the office, he was talking casually to a young man in his early twenties. "The largest information center in Europe is located in Geneva, Switzerland. I'm going to go there if I don't hear something in a day or two. Why don't you come along with me?" It sounded like a good idea to Henryk, and two days later they boarded a train bound for Geneva. Traveling for the young men would not be in the accepted fashion. They rode on the roof of the train and arrived at their destination begrimed by smoke from the engine.

In Switzerland the news was the same — bad. No word of his parents had been received from the souces available to the center in Geneva. What he did find was information about other offices that might have some clue to their fate. For the next several months he would find his home on train roofs, in boxcars, and sitting crammed into Red Cross offices with fellow seekers.

Henryk looped Europe on his odyssey. From Switzerland, he swung down into Italy, where a large concentration of Jews was located. Many Jews from Poland had gone there during the latter stages of the war via the escape routes through Hungary and Yugoslavia. Those refugees hoped to arrange passage to Israel by way of Italy. Some 15,000 Jews had been smuggled into the country before the British moved against the effort and refused to allow further transit toward Palestine. Their closing of the border had stranded another twelve thousand in Graz, Austria. Consequently, Italy and Austria were fertile areas in which to seek displaced Jews. Henryk sought information in Rome, Florence, Milan, and Naples, all to no avail.

France was the next stop along the way. Results there proved negative, as they had in Italy and Switzerland. His railbound travel would direct him to Germany and stops at Frankfurt-am-Main, Hamburg, and Munich. At each center he left an address in Warsaw where he could be contacted. By the time he departed Prague, Czechoslovakia, for the return trip to Poland, Henryk was a disheartened young man. A faint hope that confirmation of his parents' survival awaited him was the only ray of light on his horizon. When he arrived in Warsaw he hurried to the home of his friends. "I'm sorry, Henryk. We have no word of your family." The words seemed to hang frozen in the air like an epitaph.

For the first time in all the years since he had last looked into the face of his mother, the question began to take on the form of a conviction—his family had perished. The conviction would not be confirmed in his mind until he had revisited the Red Cross center in Warsaw and waited several more weeks for word from the countries he had been in. In the end, he could only arrive at the conclusion that their names must be placed in the column alongside the three million others who had died at the hands of the Nazis in Poland. He no longer expected to hear of their being alive.

For Henryk now, his entire life seemed to have been cast against a backdrop of sheer futility. He felt enmeshed in a recurring nightmare that cycled through one horrible tragedy after another. He wondered if there would ever be an avenue of escape open to him. Surpassing every other consideration at this point in his life was the fact that Henryk Weichert had been left without hope. All past adversity had been tempered by the hope of eventual reunion with his own. With that hope gone, something died within him. He had heard people talk about God—some had even called on Him during the dark days of the occupation. But how could he place any credence in the claim of the existence of a God who had left him with no hope? A God who, if He existed at all, only mocked him with one destructive disappointment after another. For weeks to come he would wander the streets of a war-ravaged city, without hope, without faith, without a shred of assurance that the future held anything better for him.

8

The Promised Land

Vwadik Jalonka warmed to the subject
with unbridled enthusiasm. A major decision had been made in his life since he and
Henryk had last been together. "I have decided to leave Poland and make a new
start," he informed his friend. "Arrangements are being made for me to go to England. I shall be leaving soon. Most of the
people who are getting out of the country
are going to Israel, but I have relatives in
England, so I am going there."

Henryk thought about it for a moment.
"What does a person have to do to leave the
country?"

"It is very simple," Vwadik replied. "A
Jewish agency has a new office here that
works in cooperation with UNRRA.* It is located in Warsaw. If you will go there, they
will make arrangements for you. Just a
minute—I'll write the address down so you
will have it."

*United Nations Relief and Rehabilitation Administration.

Henryk's mind was working while his friend wrote the address. There was no longer any reason for him to remain in Poland. The possibility of an opportunity to leave the country came as welcome news. Although he could not explain why, his mind was immediately settled on where he wanted to go. Israel, he had heard, was the land of promise. He would go there in search of what he had lost in the country of his birth. He would make his new home in a new land.

Thousands of European Jews were making the same decision as Henryk. The war was over, but persecution of Jews had not subsided. They were ready to turn their backs once and for all on their tormentors. Between 1946 and 1948, a quarter million Jews would leave Eastern Europe. Immigration to Israel was still almost exclusively an illegal enterprise. The British mandatory government had slowed the rate of sanctioned immigration to a comparative trickle. Where the British occupation forces were active in Europe, they did what they could to circumvent the entry of Jews into Palestine. Closing the Italian frontier was an illustration of the new policy.

In spite of that, however, many escape routes were kept open that eventually deposited refugees on the beaches of Italy, France, Rumania, Yugoslavia, and Greece.

There they were loaded aboard leaky tubs, which passed for transport vessels, for the voyage to Israel. For the vast majority of those who made the trip, it was a journey into more troubled waters. The British relentlessly hunted them down and shuttled captured passengers off to internment centers in Europe or on the island of Cyprus. Between 1945 and 1948, sixty-five of those immigrant boats would embark for Palestine.

Official sources in governments and various independent agencies defied the British dictum and cooperated with the clandestine efforts to find a national haven for embattled Jewry. The Polish government, particularly after the pogrom at Kielce, was fearful that they could not restrain further violent outbursts against Jews. Consequently, they saw emigration as a desirable solution and assisted in the exodus of Jews from their country. Czechoslovakia agreed not to hinder the mass movements, and went so far as to pay train fares for Jews fleeing from Poland. Other governments and the occupation forces of the major powers actively or tacitly gave their approval to the operation.

UNRRA, under its first director general, Herbert Lehman, was instrumental in assisting the financing of the flight of Jewish people. Among Jews themselves, groups like the Jewish Agency and the American

Jewish Joint Distribution Committee provided funding and assistance to the refugees.

Operationally, a movement called *Berihah* (flight) was the first to move people illegally across borders and toward Israel. Other Zionist groups would join the effort as time went on. The Jewish Brigade soldiers, Haganah, and Mosad moved fellow Jews along escape routes and onto the "illegal" ships.

As the struggle for recognition of statehood for Israel escalated, political groups began to recruit personnel for their movements. David Ben Gurion's Haganah, Menachem Begin's Irgun and Lohamei Herut Israel (Lehi) were actively participating in recruitment, transportation, and training of European Jews for their respective organizations.

"So you wish to go to Israel." A bald, bespectacled man was seated behind a battered desk interviewing the young prospect for the Promised Land.

"Yes, I want to leave Poland. A friend of mine told me that it could be arranged, if I would come here to your office."

"Does your family live here in Warsaw?" the man questioned.

"My parents, brothers, and sister are all dead. They died during the war. I am the only one in my family who is left."

"Unfortunately, yours is a story I hear many times each day. I deeply regret that I can do nothing about the past, but I can help you with your future. If you wish to go to Israel, it can be arranged. Take a seat over there, and wait until you are called."

Henryk waited with the other applicants until his name was called by a young woman who held some papers in her hand. She issued him an UNRRA Refugee Card and gave him instructions about the date and time he could expect to leave Warsaw. On the appointed day he assembled with a number of Jewish people who were making the first leg of the trip along with him. Their journey would take them to Lampertheim, a German town located near Mannheim.

Pleasant surroundings awaited the new arrivals from Poland. Their group was broken into small units that were moved into houses formerly occupied by German families. Meals were served in a central kitchen, where a festive communal air prevailed. A large segment of those who had made the trip with Henryk were young people. They all expected the stay in Lampertheim to be but a brief way station on the road to Palestine. It would be the better part of a year, however, before they moved to the next stop on their way to a new life.

Physically and psychologically, it was a constructive time for all of the six hundred

Jewish transients. An optimistic mood was the prevalent theme of life during their stay in Germany. They were constantly admonished to look ahead. For the first time in years, these people had a future. Whatever had befallen them in bygone days, there was assuredly something to anticipate now. Most of them had come out of the war heavily scarred by their experiences, so it took a while for abject despair to be set aside in favor of expectation. Gradually, the transformation began to take place. Smiles showed on faces more often. Some who had been secretive and reclusive began to communicate openly with other members of the group.

Perhaps the most obvious manifestation of change was the perceptible transference that took place. The refugees had come from families that had been ravaged by untimely and horrible deaths. When they fled Poland, the emptiness left by their losses was almost intolerable. But now, with the passage of time, they began to make friends. Those relationships would begin to fill the awful void left in their lives. If they could no longer turn to their families, they could at least turn to the familiar face of a good friend—someone who also needed understanding and companionship.

Henryk Weichert was, by the nature of his basic constitution, an outgoing individual.

He was a young man who needed friends, and, very soon, the friends he made found that they needed him. In a real sense, during that year of waiting, Henryk would begin to piece things back together again. It was, for him, the infancy of a progression—one that would see his life changed irrevocably, and as an ultimate result exercise an incredible influence on hundreds of his beloved countrymen.

As their stay in Germany drew to a close, impatience was beginning to set in. A cheer went up from the group when the announcement was made instructing them to prepare to leave their quarters for the trip to Grenoble, France.

The stay in Grenoble lasted only a few days. As the time of their departure for the coast approached, a general meeting was called to give them a briefing about the journey. The man who stood to address them was articulate and exuded optimism. He was a representative of the Irgun and would accompany the refugees to Israel, along with several other members of the organization who had joined the travelers in Grenoble.

"Tomorrow, we will leave to begin our journey to the Promised Land, Israel. It is the land of our fathers, given by God long ago to Abraham and his children.

"Many of our Jewish brothers and sisters

have already gone on before us and are waiting to receive us. When we arrive in a few days, you will be welcomed by them with open arms. You will be housed and taken care of by our friends who await us in our homeland.

"Very soon, we believe, Israel will be the national home for Jews from around the world. You have the privilege of being among those who will make the dream of a Jewish state in Palestine come true.

"We have a good, sound ship waiting to take us to Israel. It will be a pleasant voyage on the Mediterranean for all of you. In a few days we will arrive on the coast of the land of milk and honey. In the meantime, enjoy yourselves—have a good trip!"

Applause followed the speaker as he turned to take his seat. It was, to their eager ears, a fine speech. Spirits were running high as the "illegals" turned in their UNRRA identification cards. If, perchance, they ran afoul of the British, there would be no sure way to trace their origin or organizational attachment. Henryk and his companions slept fitfully that night. They were taking a long step, one that would separate them from the scene of their desperate struggle for survival. They were leaving many memories, good and bad, behind them.

When the trucks rolled into camp the next day, all the voyagers had long since been packed and assembled for their ride to the coast. Most of them had never taken an ocean voyage before. The fever of adventure was on them all. That fever would subside somewhat when they had their first glimpse of the "good, sound ship waiting to take us to Israel." It was anchored off a secluded beach in the south of France. Actually, they discovered with considerable consternation, it was not a ship at all, but a fair-sized fishing boat. That instrument of their passage to the Promised Land appeared as though it could accommodate approximately one hundred people comfortably. Six hundred bodies waited on the beach to be transported to the vessel.

They were taken on board a few at a time. Their personal belongings were stowed below deck. Sitting pressed together in cramped space on the deck of the boat, the immigrants waited for the crew members to raise the anchor and set the small craft in motion. Before that was done, the captain issued a warning that because of the number of people aboard, it would be essential for the weight to remain evenly distributed at all times. Any sudden shift of an appreciable number of persons from one side of the ship to the other could place them in danger of capsizing. All hands must resolve to hold firmly to the places they occupied on the deck.

As the boat, loaded to the limit with its expectant human cargo, moved out into the harbor, young Jewish eyes looked anxiously at the faces surrounding them. Their journey to the Promised Land had begun.

9

S.O.S.

Henryk estimated that the journey to the shores of Israel would take four or five days. The early hours of the trip were spent adjusting to the new environment. Sea air washed the deck and rigging with invigorating freshness, carrying the aroma of a new beginning. Some who were seated aft watched silently as the boat's wake sent a lazy trail of wavelets fanning out behind them. The Mediterranean was, they agreed, the most beautiful azure expanse of water on the face of the planet. As if it were taking pains to return their compliment, the sea rested beneath the ship's keel with a stillness befitting some placid inland lake.

Mastery of the art of moving about an overburdened vessel was a study in choreographic precision. Some were up while others were down. Movements to the starboard would be deftly counterbalanced by people shifting to the port side of the craft. Three positions were available to the passengers: standing, sitting, or attempting to stretch out in a relatively prone position. All three postures were exercised, for the most part, within the limited confines of an area of the deck each had claimed as his domain.

Even the temperature seemed eager to please the novice seafarers. It was early summer, but the sun seemed to fall with muted softness upon the ship. Young faces, with eyes closed, were turned toward the sky to catch the warmth sent to them by the master of the heavens. Late that evening, they watched a brilliant orange sun being slowly extinguished as it dipped beneath the sea line spanning the western horizon. Many of them were so captivated by the pink canopy magnificently tinting a few gliding clouds, that they momentarily forgot the food that was before them. As darkness enveloped the boat, someone lifted the soft strains of a familiar song. One by one other passengers joined in, until the melody was sent lilting across the surface of the quiet Mediterranean.

Henryk and some of his shipmates talked far into the night about the future. Most, it seemed, wanted to move out into a kibbutz and make their way by working the soil of their new land. Somehow the farmer's life did not catch Henryk's fancy. He had been forced to do a great deal of night harvesting during his years of personal exile. Memories of frigid barns, rodent-infested strawstacks, and lice-laden summers had dampened the romance of the pastoral life for him, No, he was basically a man who was cut out for the city. He would learn a skill when he arrived in Israel, and settle into a quiet life near one of the centers of trade and activity.

The pleasant routine established during the first day of the journey prevailed through the early stages of their voyage. On the fourth day out, a radical change was in the wind. The elements suddenly revoked their silence, as blue skies were transformed to a sullen lead gray. Scudding clouds began to move at low altitude toward the ship. The passengers became aware of a freshening gale that caused the gentle roll of the waves to mount into unsettling choppy swells. As the hours wore on, torrential rains began sweeping over the exposed travelers. The captain offered words of assurance to the inexperienced members of the party. "This frequently occurs when one is traveling on the sea. Our ship is sturdy; it was built for this sort of thing. Be calm—there is nothing to worry about. Just stay in your places; the storm will soon pass."

His listeners could not help observing that although he spoke confidently, he kept turning a wary eye toward the incoming waves.

Their captain's confidence rested on faulty intuitive optimism. Wind and sea ignored the pleas of the worried passengers and struck the boat with awesome fury. A storm that had been predicted to last no more than a few hours dragged on for days. Occasionally, the deafening assaults experienced a transition to reduced velocity, which momentarily buoyed the hopes of the beleaguered voyagers. Each fickle interlude dissolved into the unleashing of another violent episode that threatened to take them all to the bottom.

At the height of the storm, towering walls of water hovered above the railings of their small haven before crashing across the bodies huddling together on the deck. The ship shuddered under the impact of the waves and began settling lower in the water. It was as if the drama of Jonah's ill-fated voyage on this same body of water were being reenacted. Unrestrained terror broke with the waves over the immigrants. It was clear to them that they were held in the grip of a desperately perilous situation. Cries and prayers were flung against the deafening wail of the tempest. People were protesting bitterly that they had been saved from the Nazis only to perish here in the sea. To aggravate matters still further, scores of passengers were reeling under the effects of the devastating nausea of sea-

sickness. They held frantically to the railings while repeatedly expelling vomit from
their quivering bodies.

The captain had joined his charges in
forming a pessimistic appraisal of their
plight. He was now convinced that the
ship's pumping apparatus could not empty
water from the lower parts of the vessel as
rapidly as the sea was forcing it in. The
boat was settling measurably, and if there
was not a change in conditions soon, she
would be swamped. He issued an order to
the radio operator to begin sending an
S.O.S. on the wireless transmitter. The man
was well apprised of the potential consequences of his action. In all probability they
would be hauled off the ship to spend
dreary months in an internment camp. That
was, he concluded, a better alternative than
death by drowning.

Henryk sensed a strange calm amid all
the hysteria by which he was surrounded.
He, along with his fellows, pondered carefully the ramifications of being snatched
from the fires of the Holocaust only to be
inundated by the angry waters of the sea.
But he was not worried about it, nor did he
feel sorry for himself, as some others
around him obviously did. He acknowledged frankly that he had no control over
the circumstances he now found himself in.
He was resigned to whatever happened.

The phrase that had become so familiar to him in other days now crossed his mind again—*what will be, will be*. After all, there was no accurate way for him to assess the future with any guaranteed degree of accuracy. Perhaps, when all was said and done, it was better this way. Having moved from one trouble to another in the past may well mean that there was only more of the same for him in the future. At least this way he would die without protracted suffering.

For hours the radio flashed the plea for rescue across the face of the troubled Mediterranean—S.O.S.—S.O.S.—S.O.S. If any vessels heard their message, none responded. The six hundred were left to the dictates of the storm.

At first, the lessening of the wind held no more promise in their minds than the other mocking respites that had offered hope, only to snatch it from them. But when it continued to diminish and the waves slackened, they began to lift up their heads. Tired bilge pumps finally began to take the play away from the waters that had invaded the struggling fishing boat. As the clouds started to break up over their heads, things were looking much better for the seaweary band of immigrants. They had never seen the stars appear as bright or warm as those that laid a glistening carpet across the heavens that night.

Days stretched into a week, as the relieved captain followed a zigzag course in his attempt to stay beyond the reach of the British patrol ships. They passed within sight of Messina on the northern tip of Sicily, at the head of the straits separating Italy and the island just off the southern extremity of the boot. As they swung around the Italian peninsula, their course took them east, past the island of Crete, then to a slightly southerly bearing that would bring them past Cyprus well to the south of the island. They were now prepared to make their dash for the coast of Israel.

The low drone of the aircraft engine was audible before anyone could see the plane. Anxious fingers pointed to the east, as everyone seemed to spot the airborne intruder at the same time. As the plane made a slow turn to assume a heading that would bring it over the vessel, the captain was yelling to his passengers. "It is a British coastal patrol plane. Get out of sight if possible. The rest of you, lie close to the deck. If we're lucky, they may think we are fishing."

The patrol plane made two passes over the ship and then flew a tight circle around her. As the craft disappeared from view, the captain quickly changed the ship's direction and strained the aging motors to the limits of their capacity. He suspected, though, that it was a vain exercise. The game was up for this plucky boatload of refugees.

Two patrol boats responded to the report from the pilot of the British plane. As they neared the ship, they separated to facilitate an approach from both sides simultaneously. The transients were instantly transformed into an enraged mob. Some sticks on board represented the only offensive weapons available to the incensed passengers. They were quickly distributed, and the would-be immigrants prepared to defend their rights as heirs of Abraham. The boat bearing the passengers bounced on the water several feet below the deck levels of the attacking vessels. The Jews were sandwiched helplessly between the British boats. As the soldiers jumped to the deck, guns in hand, the infuriated travelers began to vent their displeasure on them. Henryk was in the middle of the melee, lustily swinging his firmly held stick at the helmeted heads of the invading adversaries. There was something about finally being on the swinging end of the club for a change that gave him a temporary sensation of satisfaction. It would not last long.

A high-pitched voice that was decidedly British was being hurled in their direction from an officer perched imperially above them. "Drop those weapons and raise your hands above your heads. Continued resistance will force us to shoot."

The captain's voice was the next one they heard above the scuffle. "Do as he says," he shouted. "It is useless to offer any further resistance."

Moans of disappointment swept through the defenders' ranks. No one knew exactly what was in store for them, but they shared a universal belief that whatever it was, it would not be good.

Their suspicion would prove to be accurate to the letter. After ten days of hoping, enduring, and hazarding their lives, the weakened band was in tow on the way to months in confinement.

Immigrants craned their necks to get a good view of the Promised Land. Haifa harbor provided the first visual exposure to Israel. It appeared from their vantage point to be a very busy place. Ships were moving in and out, and the docks were alive with people.

The captain was given orders to berth the ship at dockside and await the arrival of a boarding party. As the people waited and watched, they shared their mutual frustration at being denied entrance into the land they had come so far to make a home in. Soon a quick-stepping contingent of British port authorities came down the pier where the ship was moored. A uniformed man wearing a large, drooping mustache barked out orders. "You will leave the ship and line up along the dock as you are instructed. Any attempt to offer resistance will be dealt with swiftly and severely. Do as you are told and you will be well treated."

Henryk and his shipmates stepped from the deck of the ship onto the first solid footing they had felt beneath them in days. They were ashore in Israel. Their arrival was, most assuredly, not what any of them had in mind when they embarked from France the better part of two weeks ago. As they were being carefully searched, each of them wondered what the next move would be.

It would not be far, at least for the next twenty-four hours. They were marched off the dock in a double column and away from the immediate area where dockside activities were carried on. A barbed wire enclosure was ready to receive them. They would spend the night confined behind the tall fence before being put on a prison ship bound for the internment camp on Cyprus the next day.

Henryk and a number of his companions sat in a circle and talked together that night. The subject of their conversation ran heavily toward the injustices to which the Jewish people were perpetually subjected. The British denial of access to the shores of Israel for displaced refugees came in for an extended verbal examination. It was generally agreed that whatever measures were deemed necessary to bring an end to the British Mandate over Palestine were undoubtedly well justified. When conditions permitted, each promised himself, he would be in the center of the conflict to establish the rights of Jewish people to live here in peace. The conversation wound down around some bold talk, which set forth possibilities for an immediate attempt to escape.

One of the men from the Irgun was in the circle. He spoke to them in quiet, reassuring tones. "You will all get your chance to fight for our land eventually. No purpose can be served by taking foolish chances now. There is much work for us all to do before we are ready for such a struggle. When we go to Cyprus, you will learn how to make the best use of yourself for your country. We will not be there forever. When we leave to come back here, we will be prepared to do our jobs."

He was aware, of couse, that the talk by the young men was more rhetoric than resolution. Their talk had been only a small act of defiance that would serve until more realistic alternatives were available to them. They had demonstrated audibly that they were not cowering under a captor's hand—thus, self-assured, they could rest the night out.

It was afternoon the next day before the ship was ready to take them on board. In due time, the authorities arrived to start them in the direction of the vessel that would transport them to the camp on Cyprus. The combination of armed guards, close confinement on a prison ship, and the thoughts of spending an undetermined amount of time behind barbed wire brought back old specters to many of the refugees. Frayed nerves began to show in the faces of the people as they walked up the gangplank.

Henryk watched the shoreline slip beyond his view. If only briefly and in confinement, it had been good to have his feet down on the soil of the place that was to be his new home. In many respects, it was a land of mystery to him. He was not conversant in biblical history, so his knowledge was sketchy at best. But there was something about the place that struck a note of homecoming in his breast. They could load him on a ship and take him away, but he would return. And when he came back, it would be to stay. Israel was his home.

10

A Home Away From Home

Cyprus, an island "whose name excites the ideas of elegance and pleasure." So wrote English historian Edward Gibbon. To the six hundred Jewish refugees who had been forcibly extracted from their little vessel, the *Ben Hecht*, Cyprus was a place that held no promise of pleasure. As for elegance, that had been relegated to a period in the dim, distant past that was far beyond their powers of recall. For Henryk and his companions, the sun-splashed island was to be a seabound prison.

British Royal Marines had planted the Union Jack in Cyprian soil in 1878. Since that time, it had been a colonial possession of the far flung empire upon which "the sun never set." By the time the British white papers that strictly limited Jewish immigration into Palestine were issued, a complex of wire-fenced detention camps had been readied to receive the illegals who were attempting to enter Israel. In August of 1946 the British began deporting immigrants to those camps. Fifty-one thousand, five hundred Israelis would pass through the gates on their journey to the land they had chosen. Two thousand infants would be born to those interned on "the rosy realm of Venus," adding to the numbers of Jews who were homeward bound.

The prisoners left the ship under the watchful eyes of armed guards. They were taken into reception quarters, where a thorough search of their persons was again made. In the course of the search, they were relieved of many of the personal items carried with them from Europe. That was a great source of distress to those who had precious little materially to show for their lives up to this point. The scene seemed all too familiar to those who had previously spent time beyond the wire.

Henryk offered words of encouragement to a frail young woman who was apparently nearing the limits of her endurance. Her body trembled as frightened eyes moved from one armed soldier to another.

"This is Poland all over again," she exclaimed. Her lips lifted a quick petition toward the ceiling of the room. "Oh, God, don't let them kill us."

"No one is going to kill anyone," Henryk

said soothingly. "They are just searching to see if we have weapons."

"That is what the Germans told us at Treblinka, too. They just sent people to take showers, and they never came back. You don't know what they might do to us."

"But these are not Germans, and you are no longer at Treblinka," Henryk continued. "You have nothing to worry about. We are all safe."

"All of that seemed to have happened so long ago," she said as she began to weep softly. "This brings it all back again—I can see the expressions on their faces."

Her brief exchange with Henryk appeared to have provided an outlet for the inner tension. She began to relax somewhat. That girl's emotional tremor was not an isolated manifestation. Scores of the internees held similar reservations about the plans the British had for them. Residual phobias would track many of them to their graves.

Present reality, thankfully, did not begin to approximate their trials while they were at the disposal of the Nazis. When the preliminary processing was completed, all six hundred were hustled off to their home away from home. A number of unattractive tin-covered barracks squatted inside the rambling fenced area assigned to them. It was a large enclosure, which relieved the anxiety of the refugees somewhat. Quarters were apportioned by lots of twenty-five people to a building.

Henryk ran an inspection of his temporary home. It was not the fine hotel in which he had spent the night back in Warsaw; but it was far superior to some of the barns he had frequented. Filthy floors could be remedied by a thorough sweeping and scrubbing. Outside, the weather was ideal. Sea breezes provided enough natural air-conditioning to maintain a comfortable climate. Within sight of the building were some tree-shaded woods. All in all, he thought, he had seen worse places.

Detainees from the *Ben Hecht* would remain on the island for more than eight months before they came up for rotation to Israel. A system had been initiated that allowed the Jewish people to establish committees charged with the responsibility of choosing seven hundred fifty persons each month for sanctioned immigration. When the time came for Henryk and his fellow seafarers to become eligible for transfer, the committee allowed the entire party to proceed to Israel together.

If the refugees had no choice but to spend the next several months in confinement, they would see to it that it would not be passed as idle time. Organizational activities abounded among the internees. Youth organizations had been formed to help prepare the immigrants for settlement endeavors when they reached Israel. One could study Hebrew, attend various meetings, and even participate in military training. Henryk particularly enjoyed the speeches made by Jewish leaders in the camp. He could keep abreast of the news coming in from Israel and the political overtones events carried with them. Speakers placed a heavy emphasis on preparing the immigrants mentally for the rigors that lay ahead of them. On one occasion, the listeners were enthralled and aroused when a speaker, who was an excellent orator, challenged them dramatically.

"Every day there are developments about us that point a finger toward irrefutable evidences that our long-cherished dream will soon become a reality. Word has reached us that the matter of statehood for Israel will soon be placed before the United Nations for a vote." The impact was obvious as an excited murmur ran through the attentive group.

"As you know, the Arabs are saying they will see to it that the nation dies at birth. They have declared that they will drive us from the land of our fathers before we can make our home there. Even as I speak, enemy forces are moving against our people who are now in Israel.

"We must give ouselves without reservation to becoming prepared to fight for our homeland. Our strength will be one which is united in spirit, will, and the ability to fight. Let each decide what his part in the struggle shall be, then move forward together to win a new life in our ancient land, or death in defense of our right to live there in peace.

"May God strengthen our hands for the great task that lies before us."

An aura of expectancy shimmered over the detainees as they applied themselves to preparation for the conflict that was in their collective future. The immigrants needed a secluded place where military instruction could be given, away from the prying gaze of the British. The barracks could not be used because the guards made routine visits that could prove disruptive for the trainees. A plan was devised to build an underground chamber where a few men could be taken at a time for instruction. A site was selected in a grove of trees, where a sharp depression offered a splendid location for the digging. It was obscured from the view of soldiers who patrolled the perimeter fence. Each evening a large group of young people would gather around the area to create a picnic atmosphere, complete with loud singing and folk dancing. As the merrymakers provided cover, select crews were busy with the excavation of the cave. When the work was finished, the immigrants had a candlelit training center where future warriors could learn their skills. Trainees were divided into shifts for their instruction sessions. The classroom was small, about nine feet square, but adequate to accommodate the small units. At the close of each teaching day, the entrance was carefully covered with camouflaging foliage.

Of course, no actual weapons were available for use in the classroom. To fill the need, rough wooden substitutes for rifles were carved out for use by the fledgling soldiers. Among items covered in the curriculum were mines, grenades, artillery, and military strategy. Henryk and his contemporaries eagerly drank in the information and manual instruction they were given. When the time came, they wanted to be fully prepared for the fight.

News of the United Nation's historic vote to partition Palestine went through the camp like a wave of high voltage electricity. Some gathered to hear the particulars.

"The vote was taken on November 29th. The tally was thirty-three in favor, thirteen against and ten abstentions. On May 14, 1948, the Mandate will end and British forces will leave Palestine. Israel will be reborn as a modern state."

Near delirium gripped the people who had waited so long for something constructive to happen to Jewry. There was a fresh look on the youthful faces of participants who joined hands to dance together in high-stepping circles and lift exuberant voices in song. After two thousand traumatic years of wandering, suffering, and waiting, there was a star on the horizon of Jewish national expectation. Coming as it did at the end of the bloodiest chapter in the pages of the human documentary, the event shone brighter still. There was no accurate measure to gauge the monument of the impact upon the intellects and emotions of those people who were nearest the center of potential benefit from the decision. It assured the fact that their period of waiting would come to a satisfactory conclusion. The awesome consideration that they would be called upon to enter immediately into a fierce confrontation, in which all of the weight of probabilities for success would be scaled against them, meant little just now. The Star of David, which emblazoned the national flag, would once more be placed beside the national standards of the members of the international community. Israel was no longer the ardent fantasy of visionary dreamers, it was soil and cities, mountains and rivers. But above everything else, it was a culmination, an end and a beginning—an end to hoping for the day when the State of Israel would be a reality;

a beginning of the opportunity to turn those hopes into concrete dimensions.

Henryk joined in the communal celebration with all the fervent enthusiasm that possessed his fellow Israelis. There was something in the news that would run very deep in the young man who had known so much rejection. In a few months at the longest, he would disembark from a ship in Haifa. When he stepped onto the soil of that land, he would begin his life as a citizen of Israel—he would belong! There he would stand on equal footing with every Jew who called Israel his home. The humiliation of being a scorned minority was to be forever buried. In Israel, he would be among his own in a truly Jewish state. It was a heady experience to drink in.

Consequences of the news of the rebirth of the state were immediately evident. The Jewish men applied themselves with a renewed verve to their military classes. Mentally, their thoughts ranged among aspirations that had been fondly constructed in the quiet of the night. People all over the camp seemed to walk faster and laugh louder, and always there was high-spirited talk of their plans and what they would do with their lives in the future.

With the arrival of the new year, Henryk and his fellow watchers were eagerly numbering the days until they would leave the island for the trip to Israel. March was hard upon them when their turn for departure came. They had made many new friends during their months on Cyprus. This time, however, parting did not have a ring of finality about it. They were happily aware of the fact that within a matter of weeks all the people who had been interned would be making the same journey. Therefore, saying their good-byes was a joyful experience for both well-wisher and traveler.

Henryk went to his barracks to pack his belongings for the trip to his new home. That evening his mind reflected on the number of times in his brief life this scene had been reenacted. He had been on the move, it seemed, for his entire life. Perhaps this would be his last journey. This time he wanted to settle down and put all his troubles behind him. How wonderful it would be, he thought, if his family could be here with him now. He sat thinking about them for a long time that night. Ruth Weichert's face repeatedly took shape in his consciousness. Henryk looked into her anguished features and heard her parting words all over again. Suddenly an impassioned surge of anger came over him. How monstrously unfair and cruel it all was. She, his father, brothers, and little Tema had never harmed anyone or anything. But they had been reckoned unworthy of life and were gone forever. For a moment he felt almost guilty for having survived. Again, as he had almost every day of his life since their parting, he would draw upon his mother's words: "Now you are a man. Be strong—be strong—be strong—" Henryk resolved to be strong enough for all of them.

Next day, he passed through the gates and walked briskly up the gangplank to the ship that was waiting to take him and his companions to Israel. He was quite willing to bid a final farewell to his home away from home.

It was springtime in Israel. A touch of the season invaded his being.

11

A New Name for a New Land

When Henryk Weichert stepped off the ship in Haifa, Israel, he entered a new world. The eighteen-year-old survivor of the Holocaust was experiencing a clean sweep. He was no longer a Polish Jew; he was now an Israeli. With the soon-to-be establishment of the state, and the subsequent implementation of the Law of the Return, his recognition as a full citizen of Israel was assured.

Not only did he have a new land, but he would receive a new name as well. "In Hebrew," he was told, "*Henryk* becomes *Zvi*. From now on, this is the name by which you will be known."

So Henryk became Zvi. He liked the sound of it. It represented graphically the symbolism of change that was taking place in his life. He had made the transition to a new land; why not have a new name to go with it?

A new land, a new name—and now a new life. He would, from the first hours ashore in Israel, enter officially into a vocation which would be an integral part of his life for the next three decades and more—Zvi became a soldier. To him and the young men who disembarked at his side, it was a matter of great pride. After years of being trodden down by the heel of military tyrants, they would share the honor of serving a cause whose only design was to insure them and their descendants a right to live unmolested lives in their own land. The noble enterprise in itself brought about an immediate transformation for these young Jews. The refugee immigrant complex was falling away like the dead of winter retreating before the green breath of a clean new April. They were now Israelis, and in a very real sense, each of them felt he had placed a firm grip on the handle of the nation's future destiny.

The new arrivals were transported south to a camp located just outside Hadera—about halfway down the coast between Haifa and Tel Aviv. Hadera had been founded as a Jewish settlement in 1890. At that time it was a swampy, malaria-ridden bog, written off as worthless by its former owners. Pioneer Jewish immigrants had drained the land and planted 750 acres of eucalyptus trees to dry the soil. Zvi and the East Europeans who accompanied him found it to be a fertile growing area dotted with lush citrus groves.

The newcomers were quartered in tents. This was a new experience for the majority of these young people, who took good-naturedly to their surroundings.

A tense situation prevailed in these pre-state days, as Israelis and Arabs geared for the war to come. Already pitched battles were being fought for control of areas considered vital to one party or the other. Only the presence of the British served as a restraint to prevent a full-scale war from breaking out. In view of the situation, the raw recruits were to be pressed into almost immediate service in the defense of Jewish settlements in the vicinity. Marauding Arab bands were harassing residents, who in turn called for armed relief to drive off the attackers.

Zvi's group had entered the country under the sponsorship of Menachem Begin's Irgun organization. At that time the Irgun was one of three groups, Haganah, Lehi, and Irgun, vying for the dominant role in the coming government. David Ben-Gurion and the Haganah were clearly the superior faction from the standpoint of personnel, influence, and numbers of arms possessed. Both dissidents, Irgun and Lehi, opposed Ben-Gurion and were particularly incensed over the boundaries laid out by the U.N. Partition

Plan, which had been agreed to in principle by Ben-Gurion and Haganah. Because of their fundamental differences, each of the three entities would function through separate operations that were often in direct conflict. Of course, Zvi and his young associates knew little about the implications of anyone's political persuasion. They were finally in Israel and quite willing to fight for her survival under any banner that provided the opportunity. Politics was inconsequential to them.

Early on the morning after their arrival, the youthful volunteers left their tents for an orientation session in an orange grove. All training would be carried on inside the veil of the shielding citrus trees. Here the recruits were introduced to the first actual firearms to be used in the field. Irgun issue during the phase was ancient Italian vintage. Their carbines were leftovers from World War I. Zvi was presented with a model that stood considerably taller than he did.

The entire operation that day was carried out in a comic opera atmosphere. The young men had come together from many European countries. Most of them had considerable difficulty communicating with one another. None of them spoke Hebrew, which compounded the problem, because Hebrew was the language in which the instructor addressed them. The young soldiers did not have the faintest idea what the instructor was trying to say to them. Therefore, all training had to be done through a crude system of signs that made minimal impressions on the men. When it was time for the actual practice of firing the weapons, they quickly learned that the weapons were capable of dealing out punishment from both ends.

The first eager volunteer stepped gingerly forward to demonstrate his prowess to the other envious trainees. His first mistake was in misinterpreting the teacher's gestures about holding the clumsy blunderbuss tightly against his shoulder—he failed to do so. The gun went off with a thunderous explosion that sent the projectile roaring away in one direction and the soldier tumbling in another. When the smoke and dust lifted, the recruit dragged himself to his feet wondering if his arm and shoulder were still connected to his body. While the remainder of the group howled with delight at his misfortune, they were developing a healthy respect for the wisdom of learning to interpret the grunts and signs of their mentor properly. By the time the instructors felt confident of their mastery of the basics, Zvi and his companions had suffered bloodied noses, ringing ears, and aching shoulders, which were quickly transformed to a deep black and blue. "I can understand now," said a bruised rifleman, "why the Italians sold those guns to us. They must want the Arabs to win the war."

Food for Israel's newest residents was not readily available in great abundance. Because of the friction between Irgun and Haganah, Haganah refused to make portions of their more plentiful stock of supplies available to Irgun. That necessitated spending a portion of each day foraging for food for the camp. Raiding English supply depots at night was a productive venture. Zvi found that his old skills were still with him. He was among the most proficient procurers in the entire encampment.

It was little more than a week after the young men had landed in Haifa when the call came for their first military adventure. Arab League countries had commissioned the Liberation Army, a volunteer force made up of units from several Arab states, to enter Israel in preparation for the war that would be declared as soon as Israel gained statehood. Syrian and Iraqi troops were the most numerous elements in the country in the early days of 1948. The British looked the other way while they were infiltrating from Transjordan and Lebanon. Liberation Army forces were scattered throughout an area known as "the triangle." Points of the triangle were Jenin in the north, Nablus in the south, and Tulkarm to the west. Arab volunteers were marking time as they awaited the arrival of the full complement of troops and their leader, Fawzi El Kawkji. Plans called for all troops to be assembled and in position by May 14, when the British were scheduled to pull out of Palestine. The minute the English evacuated, they would begin their grand push to sweep the sons of Jacob into the sea. Advance contingents proposed to live off the spoils taken from Jewish settlements in the area—thus the crisis that brought distress to the settlers in the vicinity of the camp at Hadera.

Leaders of the Irgun conferred and decided to attack the Arabs at Tulkarm, the western point of the triangle located roughly fifteen miles from the tent homes of the immigrants.

The march to their first battle was begun with high-spirited enthusiasm. Immigrant boys went to face their enemies as young men always do in the early days of war. They were convinced that their foe was no match for them. As they moved along the road, one of Zvi's companions was speculating about the encounter.

"The Arabs will not like what we have for them," he boasted. "They will probably turn and run when they see us coming."

"If they don't, it will be their funeral," predicted another.

"I have heard that Arabs will not stand and fight," said a third. "They will throw a few shots in your direction, then get away."

The first soldier had a second observation. "I'll tell you what they are good at: stealing from women and shooting old men in the back. They won't be so brave when they are up against men who know how to fight."

A wave of agreement swept through the ranks of the untested combatants.

Their bravado cooled as they approached Tulkarm. By the time they reached the scene of the attack, they were stone quiet and visibly shaken by the prospect of being shot at. They were, after all, just boys who were participants in a cruel enterprise.

Arabs were caught off guard by the opening volley, and for a time it looked as though the Jewish attackers would enjoy a measure of success in their initial test under fire. That illusion was shattered in a hail of bullets streaming from the superior weapons of the Arabs. The refugees' rifles were cumbersome and inaccurate. Soon the screams of the wounded joined the whine of bullets over the battlefield. It was immediately apparent that the attackers were no match for the defenders—the call to retreat was issued.

Zvi helped drag a wounded youth out of the range of Arab guns. The boy was bleeding profusely from a wound in the upper chest. As he was returning to aid another comrade, he came upon one of their number who had been hit in a vital organ and died within seconds after he had fallen. The expression on the dead boy's face struck Zvi as being one of complete astonishment. It was as though, even in death, he could not believe he would come so far and die so soon. Zvi was no stranger to the pale face of death. But there was something about the quality of death in this place that added a particular hideousness to the act. Those who were taken away from the fight for burial were not emaciated hulks with drawn faces. These were healthy bodies which only moments before had been looking ahead expectantly to the rest of their lives. Yes, he thought, death had a different face here in Israel.

It was a solemn band of soldiers who filed back into the camp to face the barrage of questions flung at them by the women who had stayed behind. They made their glum reports and accepted the words of condolence and encouragement. A first taste of battle had served to season them. They had faced their enemy and found him to be a determined fighter. Now they understood that the price of independence for Israel would come high in terms of personal sacrifice. Each of them fervently hoped the price he paid would not be his life.

Over the next few weeks some of their friends would be called on to pay the highest toll exacted from men of war. Skirmishes were fought over the area in an effort to relieve the pressure on the beleaguered settlements. In each instance their assaults were repulsed by the enemy, and they were sent away without tasting victory.

Those were rather curious confrontations, because the Jews had two hostile forces to contend with. While they were exchanging shots with the Arabs, there was always the necessity to keep a wary eye out for the British. When the emissaries of the crown would be within earshot of a battle and hasten to the scene, the Jewish fighters would be forced to turn on their heels and flee. The problem then was to avoid death from the Arab guns and capture by the British.

As the date that had been set for the British withdrawal neared, Zvi's group took up positions in a mountainous region where they occupied fire positions and did observation duty. A primary objective was to stay out of the reach of the English and prepare for the impending struggle.

During those last decisive days of waiting, an important climax was in the making that would change the makeup of the armed forces of Israel. On April 25, Irgun troops made a frontal assault on Manshiya, a section of Jaffa near the center of Tel Aviv. This move has been interpreted as an effort by Irgun to make a big push to gain recognition as a military force before the Jewish population. An Irgun success would reflect negatively on Haganah and damage their prestige as Israel's premier fighting unit. In preparation for the attack, hundreds of Irgun's best personnel were brought in from other parts of the country to join the operation.

The attack was launched early in the morning and met with little success that day or early the next. Consequently, the Irgun High Command felt it was time to make renewed overtures to the leadership of Haganah. Begin's proposal for a unified command was accepted. The agreement went into effect the same evening, April 26. Haganah area commanders were instructed, "This is to inform you that wherever there are Irgun positions, they will from now on come under the command of Haganah."

Zvi was now a member of the group that would become the Israel Defense Force — the army of Israel.

Already, strategy was being developed for one of the first major confrontations after the British withdrawal from the country. Arabs had succeeded in closing the Tel Aviv-Jerusalem Road — a move that placed the Jewish population in the City of David in great peril. Food stores for the residents were being depleted. That condition necessitated immediate action to relieve and resupply the city. Jews would attack the Arabs at Latrun, the strongpoint dominating the road to Jerusalem.

Zvi and his unit swung into position to join the battle.

12

No Place To Hide

"Take Latrun!" David Ben-Gurion was issuing very specific orders to Yigal Yadin. Yadin was in charge of all Haganah military operations in Israel. He had argued vehemently against an attack at Latrun just now. Yadin felt that if there were to be any realistic hope of success, he must have more time to prepare for the engagement.

In fact, Yigal Yadin had good cause to be apprehensive about the operation. Israel had been a state for less than ten days when he received the order to capture Latrun. Already a flood of invading Arab forces was flowing into Israel to complement those who had previously infiltrated the borders established by the United Nations partition plan. There was not sufficient fire power available to Yadin's men; nor did he have enough trained troops to staff the operation. Besides those formidable difficulties, the paper-thin line of Jewish soldiers under his command was under attack in many parts of the country he considered more strategic at the moment than Latrun.

Ben-Gurion would not be swayed. If any portion of Jerusalem was to remain under Jewish control, supplies must be brought in immediately. In his view, a Jewish presence in Jerusalem meant life or death for the infant nation. If Jerusalem fell, he argued, it would cause people to be demoralized to the point of losing heart in the struggle for independence. Failure to move the convoys up the Tel Aviv-Jerusalem Road to save the city would probably mean the death of the nation. There was no other choice.

Now that the final decision had been made, the problem became strictly a military one. Latrun sat astride what was, at this time, the most important crossroads in the Middle East. It was located at a point where the Tel Aviv-Jerusalem Road intersected with a road running north to Ramallah and south to the ancient port city of Ashkelon. Commanding the dominant rise on the northern side of the Jerusalem Road stood a large police station that had been abandoned by the British. Only days before the attack was to be made, the police station had been occupied by a small Jewish force. They had been driven off by Arabs who were now in firm control of the fortresslike brown building. While Zvi and his fellow Jews were preparing for the job ahead of them, contingents of the Fourth Battalion of the Jordanian Arab Legion were digging in at Latrun to repel the attack. The Arab legionnaires were crack troops, trained, equipped, and sometimes led by British officers.

On the slopes descending toward the road, Arab soldiers were busy implanting a network of machine-gun implacements. Any attacking army would find it necessary to cross the wide expanse of open fields squarely into the teeth of those guns. While the machine guns were being situated, others were opening old trenches that had been used by Turkish troops to defend the position against General Edmund Allenby's British force in 1917. High caliber machine guns were placed on the roof of the police headquarters, a position that provided a commanding view of the entire area. Barbed wire was uncoiled along the slope to further impede the progress of charging soldiers. Antitank guns were deployed at strategic points to add to the discomfiture of the Jewish lads who were expected to pay a call.

Five miles away, at Hulda, Jewish troops were being brought to a staging area in buses. Hulda was the last Jewish settlement between Tel Aviv and Latrun. This force was made up of two Israeli contingents charged with capturing the crossroads and liberating Jerusalem. The Alexandroni Battalion was a veteran unit made up of seasoned Palmach troops, a capable, battle-hardened group of men who knew how to conduct themselves on the field of battle. Zvi was a member of the companion battalion, the "New Brigade." Although Zvi had been in the country only a matter of weeks, he was considered a veteran in the New Brigade battalion, which was made up of immigrants. They came from many European countries, and shared, as had Zvi's orange-grove companions, the problem of the language barrier. A large number of those men had been brought to the Hulda staging area fresh off the docks in Haifa—they had been in Israel only a matter of hours. Most had little or no training in firing the rifles they were issued. Some did not even know how to release the safety mechanisms on their weapons. In addition to those obvious handicaps, they left the buses without helmets, water containers, or field packs. For the most part, their training would consist of a cram course in a few Hebrew commands and some quick words about the use of the guns.

In view of the desperate urgency that dictated priorities at this stage of the war for independence, Jewish leaders had few other options open to them. Untested men must be thrust into the heart of the battles, in the hope that military miracles might somehow be wrought.

As midnight, the hour scheduled for the attack, neared, the men were moved from Hulda to the jumping-off point two and a half miles below Latrun. As they came into position for the march toward the crossroads, the men stood viewing a spectacular panorama. Stretching out before them lay the fertile Alayon Valley. The moon cast a brilliant illumination over the vale that gave the scene a gauzy silver appearance. Ripened wheat stood knee deep in the rich soil. There was not a quiver of air moving that night. The entire valley seemed to be holding its breath in anticipation of what lay ahead.

As the nervous immigrants awaited the order to move out, Zvi was engrossed in a conversation with a religious Jew from Poland.

"Did you know you are standing now before a very famous place?" said the student of the Bible.

"Famous in what way?" asked Zvi.

"How well do you know the Bible?" his friend queried.

"I don't read the Bible," Zvi replied.

"Well then I will tell you. At this place, God brought about a miracle and gave our fathers a great victory.

"It was in the days of Joshua, after our

people had come out of Egypt. The kings of the Amorites formed an alliance against Israel and brought their army to this place. Joshua and his men fought hard against them until the battle started to go in his favor. Then Joshua commanded the sun to stand still in the heavens until the battle could be fully won. God heard him, and the sun did not move across the sky for a day. This is spoken of in the Bible. It says there was no day like it before, because the Lord fought for Israel that day.

"I believe God will fight here for Israel tonight. I am sure he will give us a great victory over our enemies, too."

"I hope you are right," Zvi said with a skeptical edge on his words, "but I don't think God has much interest in what goes on here now."

Their talk was cut short by the order to move into the valley and proceed toward Latrun. They walked as quietly as possible. The slim chance open to them for victory hung delicately balanced on the fulcrum of the element of surprise. By four in the morning they were drawing abreast of their destination. Soon the attack would be launched.

The miracle that had come to the aid of Joshua and his host was not extended to Israel's modern men of war. An Arab lieutenant would be the source of their undoing.

Quite by chance, he was out on the road that night returning to his station. Through the moonlight, he caught sight of the Jewish troops as they moved cautiously through the wheat fields. He snatched up his radio transmitter to inform his superiors of the imminent attack.

The entire hillside before the Jews suddenly erupted in their faces. Before they had fired a shot, their ranks were ripped by a whirlwind of metal-cased destruction. As the sounds of gunfire echoed across the valley, Arab villagers living nearby ran from their homes to join the legionnaries who were destroying the Jewish force.

Zvi saw several immigrants around him fall before the first withering volley. He and his overwhelmed fellows hit the ground and began looking for cover. To their dismay, there was no place to hide. The terrain on the slope before them offered few possibilities for protection. The best they could do was hug the ground and hope for help to come from some other quarter.

As the sun came up over Alayon, a new enemy marched on the scene. A wave of unbearable heat enveloped the valley and soon turned it into an oven of torment. Compounding their misery was an invasion by thousands of tiny mosquitoes that relentlessly assailed every exposed area of the men's bodies.

Before ordering a general retreat, the commanders attempted a flanking action, which they hoped would relieve the pressure on the trapped soldiers. The attack was turned aside by a shower of heavy machine-gun fire from the roof of the police station. When the retreat was called, the men encountered the agony of trying to outrun the bullets and the whizzing pieces of lethal shrapnel that flew through the air. Each time the young Jews began to rise and continue their effort to retreat, the Arab guns tore them apart. Shouts and groans from the wounded hung in the still, torrid air above the wheatfields, which were now ablaze about them.

As the day wore on, many fell prey to the effects of the sun. They were maddened by thirst and the swarming insects. Zvi was among those who kept trying to drag wounded comrades to the scant cover to be found in the fields. The sun scorched his head as heatwaves danced off the valley floor to mingle with the smoke and noise. Men fell spewing blood from gaping holes that had been torn in their bodies. Suddenly, he saw a sight that momentarily froze his senses. Arab villagers were running among the fallen Jews, pausing long enough to bend over the wounded and repeatedly plunge daggers into their helpless bodies.

Finally, numb with exhaustion, crazed by thirst, and engulfed in the deafening sounds of war crashing about him, he didn't care anymore. He got to his feet and started away from the sound of the guns. Zvi could hear the high-pitched whine of the bullets as they passed within inches of his body. But try as they would, none of the Arab riflemen could find the mark.

His course carried him toward the village of Beit Jiz. There, he had been told, they would find water and transportation for the trip back to their camp. All he found when he arrived were more Arab guns spewing death on the approaching Jewish soldiers. He paused for a moment to survey the incredible scenes being enacted around him. Men were staggering about as though they did not know which direction to go in search of safety. Some were on the ground, begging to be shot by their own men and put out of their suffering. Officers were pushing, cajoling, and physically beating the men to get them to their feet and out of the range of enemy guns.

If, he thought, an artist had conceived a picture of hell, he could imagine nothing closer to reality than what was passing before his burning eyes. Horrible beyond imagination, it was like a compressed version of the Holocaust over again—a cauldron of devastation.

In actuality, he was not overplaying the scene. Losses incurred by those raw troops at Latrun would be the heaviest concentration of casualties suffered by Israeli Defense Forces over the span of three wars. An Arab officer would enunciate a striking oral epitaph during the victory celebration following the battle, "I have before me the identity cards of Jews from many nationalities who have come to this country from the ends of the earth." Some, who had been in the land of promise less than seventy-two hours, came from the ends of the earth to die in the smouldering wheatfields of Latrun.

It was mid-afternoon before a few battered remnants of the Jewish strike force came reeling back to the original assembly point. Slowly, the stunned fragments of the broken unit wandered to the buses for the trip away from the scene of their defeat.

Zvi left the bus but did not tumble into his bunk as the others did. Instead he walked to a secluded place and dropped down under the covering branches of a low-hanging tree. He was covered with the grime of the battlefield. His face had been seared by the acrid smoke he had fought during the morning hours. Here and there, his uniform was smeared with the blood of wounded comrades he had assisted during the battle. This was clearly not the young man who had entered the battle with fresh garments and high hopes for victory. What was perceptibly true on the outside was in the process of becoming an indelible reality within him. Young Zvi was in the grip of a dynamic inward transformation.

It was not as though the sun had hung motionless at his command in the heavens in some breathtaking display of divine affirmation, as it had in Joshua's long-gone day. But there in Ayalon's vale, a revelation of another kind had become crystal clear in his mind. There in the stillness of the evening, his thoughts moved carefully back across the years. The painful scenes of his childhood and early years were vividly framed before him. The orphanage days, the German decision to send him back to Poland, bullets passing close as he fled from the ghetto, his escape from the German who was determined to kill him, survival after the Nazis had beaten him almost lifeless, the daily groveling for enough food to sustain a semblance of life, seas rising and falling with death written across every whitecap, and then today.

Until today, he had viewed his tenacious hold on life as a product of his own ingenuity. He was always just a little too smart for them, or a bit too quick for them. While others died pathetically about him, Zvi could live by his wits. He would prevail while others could not. No matter what the odds against him had been, he could make it.

Today, he knew that he had been a fool all along—an overconfident, arrogant fool. Today, he should have died. Today, he knew many times that he was sure to meet death. Today, he had stood within reach of those who had been cut down by the sickle of death. Today, he had stood up and treated death with disdain—exposed his body to enemy fire. Today, he had not met death.

Zvi could not delude himself any longer. It was not, he knew, his strength, quickness, or wits that had delivered him at nearly every turn in the road. How foolish he had been not to see it. There could be one answer and one answer only—it was God! It could be only God.

How strange it seemed to him even to utter the name of God. He had not been brought up in a religious home; he had had no attachment to the synagogue, nor had he acknowledged God or sought Him during the days of his distress in Europe. He had always been too busy saving his life or congratulating himself for doing so. But now he was convinced, as he was of his presence beneath the tree, that God alone had been his constant protector and deliverer.

There was another realization of which he was now quite positive: God had spared him for a purpose. He had not lived because he was more intelligent, gifted, or worthy than the millions who had died about him. He was sure of that. But he was also sure that somewhere in the mystery that engulfed God in his awakening mind at this time, there was a purpose for his continuing existence. God had something for him to do.

Now the question was how to find the Lord and how to know what He expected of him. The vast void that had occupied Zvi's soul since the day he had become convinced his family had perished was replaced by a consuming hunger—a hunger to know God.

Amidst the clatter and confusion that was Latrun, Jehovah had arrested the attention of one frail son of Abraham—one to whom He purposed to reveal Himself and in whom He wished to take up residence. In a sense, it was as much a miracle as had been granted to Zvi's forebear, Joshua. On this occasion it was not the sun which stood riveted immobile in the heavens, but one young man who stood mute before his God. In the silence of that singular act, he had acknowledged the existence of God and his dependence upon Him. From that day forward, Zvi would follow an unfolding progression, one that would ultimately—inexorably—bring him to the place where his hunger could be satisfied.

Zvi's religious friend had his miracle. Not

in the way he expected it to come—he was not even personally aware that it had transpired—but he had it nonetheless. The Jews had lost one battle; God had won the initial engagement in a campaign for a man's soul. It was a victory of miraculous magnitude.

Before he slept that night, Zvi arrived at one more conclusion. In the valley of Ayalon that day, before the death-dealing guns of Latrun, he had searched but found no place to hide. Likewise, he affirmed, there was no place on earth for a man to hide from his God.

13

You Get One Mistake

"He is a man who appears to have what it takes for the job," the officer said.

"Yes," agreed his superior. "I saw him in the field while the battle was going on. He is very quick and appears to be totally fearless.

"You talk to him and see if you can persuade him to do it."

Within a few hours, Zvi had been beckoned to the young Haganah officer's quarters for a tête-à-tête. As he walked to the meeting, he wondered what he had done to be called in for a personal conference.

"We've been watching you and feel you are qualified to do something for us," the officer began.

"Thank you," said the blond soldier. "I'm glad I am doing my job well."

The officer came to the point. "How would you like to take special training for a good job?" he asked.

Those words had a familiar ring to Zvi. He remembered another occasion when a handsome partisan had used similar terminology. This time he would ask a question or two before he took the bait.

"May I ask what kind of job you have for me?" he inquired.

"It is a very important one, which few men can do. One who can do this properly will save many lives and serve his country with great honor.

"We want you to work with mines. Do you know about them?"

"Not much," the prospect replied. "They told us about them while I was on Cyprus and in the orange groves, but I can't say that I learned a great deal."

"Would you like to train for the job?" the officer concluded.

"Yes, I will do it."

"Good. There is a training camp near Netanyah. You will be taken there tomorrow."

So Zvi was enlisted in one of the most dangerous occupations any soldier undertakes. During the next thirty years he would remove and defuse thousands of mines, booby traps, and other potentially lethal devices planted by Arab armies and terrorists.

The opening statement of his instructor at Netanyah made a lasting impression on him.

"You are going into an interesting business; one you will have just cause to be proud in doing well. This is the only department in the army of Israel where you must do a perfect job every time. When you are working with mines, you only get one mistake. You will not get the chance to make the same error twice."

Zvi listened and wondered if he had chosen the right vocation. Latrun had brought about a profound change in his attitude toward life. His courage and devotion to duty remained unshaken, but he was no longer foolhardy. He would take necessary risks in the line of proper service, yet he would no longer dare death to take him. In a sense, his life was still barren and empty. He had not found fulfillment, but he now realized that God had brought him this far. He would not risk God's property unnecessarily.

When he returned to his unit, after a few days in Netanyah, he found they had moved to the Jerusalem sector. He followed them to join his command there and help keep David Ben-Gurion's dream of a Jewish Jerusalem alive.

The Holy City was divided in two sections when he arrived on the scene; eastern and western. Arabs held the eastern portion, which included the Old City. Jews had a precarious hold on the western side and a small enclave on Mount Scopus, where the

Hebrew University and Hadassah Hospital were located.

The Arabs were executing a two-pronged offensive designed to crush military resistance in the general area surrounding Jerusalem while starving the residents of the city into submission. The latter consideration made it imperative that they keep the Jerusalem-Tel Aviv Road closed to supply convoys. As had been repeated with such devastating regularity throughout history, the City of Peace was under siege by a hostile aggressor.

While army and civilian volunteers labored frantically to construct an alternate supply route to Jerusalem, Zvi and his comrades had their hands full with the representatives of the Arab Legion—the unit they had been so rudely introduced to at Latrun. Fierce fighting was going on around Mount Zion, as Jewish forces attempted to secure a strong position there. Zvi was thrown into the fray immediately. Every night, he and fellow demolition experts were out removing mines and planting explosives in an attempt to dislodge their stubborn enemies. Crossing from the Jewish sector to Mount Zion was an impossible enterprise during daylight hours. The Arab Legion troops who manned the wall of the Old City had a commanding view of the approaches to Zion's summit. Any movement drew an extended fusilade from the legionnaires.

Zvi's group managed to string a wire across the Hinnon, over which they could ferry supplies to areas that were sheltered from the riflemen on the walls. When it was time for operations to begin at night, they would slip across the Hinnon and retrieve the explosives for their night's work.

Zvi was thankful to have a close friend to assist him during his days of initiation as a mine extractor. He had met David at the training center in Netanyah. The two trainees struck up an instant association that turned into a warm relationship. David was a native Jerusalemite, a sabra, whose parents had come to Israel from Iraq as young immigrants. Since their arrival in the beloved city, they had been blessed with ten children. David was the eldest.

Having been raised in Jerusalem, Zvi's young friend had a tremendous advantage over the new immigrant from Poland. He knew every nook and cranny about the city and could lead expeditions through the darkness with unerring accuracy. On many occasions, Zvi was prevented from taking routes that would have led him into disaster by his young companion's knowledge of the territory.

After several hard days of fighting, during which all the combatants were constantly on the brink of exhaustion, a truce was called. Although there was still much for Zvi's group to do, he now had the opportunity to pause and take a good look at Jerusalem.

He liked what he saw. Zvi had never, in all of his travels in Europe, seen anything comparable to the city of his ancestor David. Viewing the massive wall and its stately ramparts left him amazed at the size and ancient grandeur with which it enveloped the Old City. Domed buildings, sharp-towered minarets, and ornate churches intrigued his youthful mind further. Just the ancient look about the city and its environs stirred his inquisitiveness and caused him to yearn for the day when the war would be over and he could pry open the mysteries of the city of his fathers.

Zvi had the same feeling about Jerusalem he had experienced when he first stepped onto the soil of Israel as a prisoner of the British. He knew at once that Jerusalem would be his home. From the moment he first saw her, Jerusalem began to spin a web tightly around the young vagabond. He was falling to the wiles of the one city in all the world that held such mystical power over the hearts of her sons and daughters. From that time on, one more Jew would say with the ancients, "If I forget thee, O Jerusalem, let my right hand forget her cunning" (Psalm 137:5).

Somehow, Zvi felt assured he would find the answers to his questions here. He had heard it called the "City of Peace." Personal peace, he hoped, awaited him there.

Zvi's friend, David, was cheerful, intelligent, and patient. Zvi would test his patience to the limit with a barrage of questions about his new home. He wanted to know about those walls—who built them and when? "What," he wondered aloud, "are those curious little crescents on the tops of the towers with the strange names? What is a Moslem? What do they do inside their mosques?" He wanted to have an explanation for there being so many religious people in odd dress about Jerusalem. "What made this a Holy City?" he wanted to know. "Explain, please, how Jews worship God in their synagogues?" he questioned.

On he would go, ad infinitum, until his belabored friend would throw up his hands and beg for mercy. "Oh, Zvi! That is enough questioning for now. You have my brain spinning like a top. Tomorrow I will take up the lesson again; tonight, let's get a little sleep."

At that, the eager student would condescendingly extend mercy and beat a temporary retreat to ponder what he had taken in that day.

Those critical days in Jerusalem in the summer of 1948 exhibited all the dark di-

mensions of war. But as it is in any protracted human experience, there were situa-
tions that produced distracting interludes.

Zvi awoke one morning in the grip of an
illness that caused him to feel nauseated
and feverish. About the middle of the morning his commanding officer came to him.
"Zvi, I don't want you to go out anywhere
this afternoon. You have an important as-
signment tonight, and I want you well
rested for what you have to do."

"I'm sorry," Zvi said. "I will not be able to
go out tonight."

"Why not?" his superior wanted to know.

"Because I feel very sick. I am afraid I will
endanger myself and the others if I go."

"I can't take that for an excuse. Sick or
not, you will have to go."

Zvi tried to explain further, but his youthful commander was adamant. The discussion turned into a full-blown argument. In
Zvi, the officer found a man who, under the
influence of a fever augmented by an injus-
tice, would be as belligerent as a tough-
minded leader of troops. Their heated exchange continued until the exasperated
private decided to make his point more
forcefully. He stooped down, picked up a
fair-sized rock, held it in both hands over his
head, and sent it crashing to the ground,
squarely upon the ankle of his antagonist.
The young debater had intended only to

make a firm impression in the ground and his commander's mind. Instead, he made quite an impression on his leader's ankle—a bone was broken.

While the officer was carried grimacing away toward the hospital, Zvi was ushered, protesting loudly, to the stockade. After a few hours of confinement, it was obvious that the soldier was a sick man. A doctor examined him and recommended a visit to the hospital for treatment. When he arrived, the bed assigned to him was located next to the officer he had injured. His superior was in a deep sleep, recovering from the ordeal of having the leg set and placed in a cast.

Zvi slept for a short time and awoke feeling somewhat better—well enough, in fact, to want something to eat. It was not near mealtime, so he began rummaging through the drawers of the table between his and the officer's beds. The hungry private found that solicitous friend of his leader had left some candy for him to enjoy during his recovery. Zvi thought he would sample some—he did. It was good enough to keep on sampling until it was gone. He was quite satisfied when he rolled over and went back to sleep.

Zvi was awakened later by the sound of visitors' voices at the bed next to his. Reluctant to face the man he had offended, he pulled the blanket up a little higher on his head and kept his face turned away. After the friends had chatted for a time, the gentleman officer wished to extend some hospitality to his guests. "Get some candy out of the drawer and pass it around," he directed one of the callers.

"What drawer?" the man questioned.

"The one you just opened," he said.

"You must have been dreaming there was candy in here," his friend replied. "This drawer is empty."

"I am not dreaming. I saw it put there with my own eyes."

The dawn broke. He looked around the ward and demanded a prompt confession from the culprit. Wide grins broke out on the faces of the sick soldiers, but no one betrayed Zvi. When the officer saw that only one face was not turned in his direction, he issued a stern command: "You! Turn this way and let me get a look at you." Zvi knew the game was up, and turned, grinning sheepishly, toward his disturbed commander. The man slapped his forehead and fell back on the bed. "Oh no!" he lamented. "It is not bad enough for you to break my leg, you have eaten my candy too."

Pandemonium swept the room. It was the funniest thing these soldiers had seen happen to an officer of the army of Israel. It was a rare moment of comic relief—one they would long remember. The young officer tried in vain to contain himself. In the end, he, too, was overcome by a fit of laughter. When he had regained control of himself, he turned on his side and thrust an outstretched hand toward Zvi—all was forgiven. The two who routinely faced death together would be lifetime friends as well.

The same officer, who was destined to rise to a high position in the Israeli government, would later prove his friendship by coming to Zvi's rescue on another occasion. Zvi and some friends from his unit had elected, on their own initiative, to extend a pass a few hours beyond the allotted time. When they returned to their post, they found an officer who was rather perturbed by their taking liberties with his instructions. He administered a swift brand of justice: "Three days in the stockade for the lot of you."

There was a saying in the army at that time that no soldier was worth his salt as a fighting man until he had spent some time in the stockade. As things were viewed from the perspective of those who occupied the lower echelons, it was the test of a genuine soldier. Upon arriving at his place of confinement, however, Zvi found the stockade not to his liking. He and his companions were put to work in a small garden, raking and doing yard duty. That evening some sympathetic members of their unit came to pay them a call.

"We came to see the convicts," his friend David said. "How do you like being locked up?"

"I can tell you, I don't like this place very much," Zvi said glumly. "I may decide not to stay the whole three days."

This drew a big laugh from the visitors. "And tell me, please," said a bright-faced young fellow, "where will you go when you leave this fine hotel?"

"I haven't made up my mind yet," Zvi informed him. "My friends and I may choose to take another day or two to see the sights."

"Ha, Zvi," David retorted, "you are like a skinny sparrow in a cage. Look at you — guards, guns, a wall. All of you will stay put until they come to you and say, 'OK boys, if you promise to be good, we will let you go.'"

The challenge implied was more than Zvi could bear. "Bring me a finger of dynamite and a detonator, and I will show you how well a skinny sparrow can fly."

"You've got it," said his cooperative friend. "Now let's see if you have the nerve to use it."

Next day, his friends returned with the dynamite. Stockade security at that stage of the development of Israel's armed forces was a rather loose affair, so there was little difficulty getting the delivery made. When their fellows departed, the escape artists huddled to lay plans. "The only thing I'm worried about," said one of the more cautious types in their company, "is that the guards have rifles. What if they should shoot us?"

"We will take care of that," Zvi assured him. "If they do what they did last night, it will be no trouble."

He was right. The guards had established a pattern of leaning their rifles against a tree while they sat around a table nearby to play cards. This was a place where men were brought for minor infractions, so the keepers of the keys were not afraid of being accosted. Consequently, it was a relatively simple matter, under the cover of darkness, to slip up to the tree and carry the weapons away. With the guns safely hidden, the sparrows went about the business of setting the charge in the wall.

The explosion went off with a dull "wump." Guards jumped straight up in alarm, and the playing cards were scattered in every direction. They ran for their guns and came up empty-handed. Next stop was the wall, which now hosted a gaping hole before which a cloud of dust was hovering. In the distant darkness, the astonished jailers could hear the laughter of the escapees as they said "good-bye" to the stockade.

A short time later the young celebrities swaggered into the camp, obviously pleased with their newly acquired notoriety. They were in the midst of an explanatory conference when the puffing guards came steaming into the camp. They went straight to the commander with a request for the return of the prisoners.

"What has happened here?" demanded the officer.

"These men blew a hole in the wall of the stockade," they complained. "They have made real trouble for themselves now."

The officer addressed the man in charge curtly. "Why didn't you stop them?"

"We couldn't," he answered.

"What do you mean, you couldn't?" he countered.

"Because they took our guns and hid them," the embarrassed soldier confessed.

"Well," said the commander, "if you allowed them to take your guns, there will be someone in the stockade tonight, but it won't be these men—it will be you!"

The man whose leg Zvi had broken looked at his subordinate with mock severity. "Get to your beds. And no more mischief, or you will understand what it means to be in trouble."

Zvi and his companions knew all too well that this sort of frivolity was but a temporary emollient that diverted attention from the sound and fury of combat. Within a matter of days the battle was on again, and their nights were occupied with plying their delicate skills.

"Zvi, I want you to come to my home today and meet my family," David was saying to his friend. The young man from Europe, who had no family of his own, counted this invitation a great honor and made preparations for the social engagement.

The two went together into the Jewish residential section of Jerusalem. They walked onto a narrow street lined with crowded living quarters. When they arrived, the father welcomed them into a room that was alive with inquisitive children. At first they looked him over from a distance with coy glances. Before long the strange visitor was the special object of their attention. Zvi drank in his newfound popularity with undisguised relish. He had not had much time to spend in happy circumstances with children, or to be one himself, and he was enjoying the attention immensely.

After a simple meal, the father shooed the children out of the room, and the three of them sat over cups of tea. "We have heard much of Zvi in this house," the father said. "I am happy, at last, to have the opportunity to meet the man who has been such a good friend to David."

"It has been my good fortune to know him," Zvi answered. "He has been a friend who has kept me out of trouble many times."

"Yes," offered his young companion, "and we have seen much of Jerusalem together during these past months."

The conversation went on late into the afternoon, and ended with warm "shaloms" and a promise to do this again before too long.

Zvi and David hurried through the streets and back to their post. Soon, they were moving out on a night mission on Mount Zion. Everything was going according to plan, as the line of men bore their explosives quietly through the darkness. They were aware of the necessity of passing close to an Arab position, but they miscalculated its exact location. Suddenly, the men found themselves almost upon the Arabs they were trying to avoid. A brisk fire fight broke out. Zvi dove behind a pile of rocks in an attempt to find some protection. Nearby, David pulled the pin from a grenade and was about to lob it into the Arab emplacement when the device malfunctioned and exploded in his hand. He was killed instantly. A distraught Zvi groped through the shadows to where David's body lay motionless, and began to drag his friend's mangled corpse down the mount amid a storm of bullets that were pelting the ground around him.

Next morning, David's body was readied for burial. Because Zvi was a close friend, he was assigned as honor bearer to the funeral party. When the bereaved father met the procession, he wilted under the burden of his grief. The man threw himself across the front of the car in which Zvi was riding and wept uncontrollably. Zvi went to him and laid a comforting hand on the man's arm. David's father turned questioning eyes toward Zvi.

"Yesterday, we sat together in my home and you promised to come there with him again. Now you are taking him to put him in the ground. No! Please bring him to his home again."

Zvi knew it could not be, and the procession moved along with the hysterical father protesting the death of his firstborn. This was a situation Zvi was totally unprepared to cope with. He wished with all his heart he could bring his dead friend back to life and return him to his anguished father. That, of course, was beyond human abilities, so he wanted only to get away from the sorrowful scene—to find some quiet place in which to retreat.

On the way back from the burial, a reflective young man was feeling his spiritual emptiness. Dying was an inevitable part of war, and Zvi was no stranger to it. But today he had witnessed the personal ramifications of death in an unsettling confrontation. He had nothing to contribute that could comfort David's distressed father in his trauma of sorrow. All he could do was feel his own helplessness as a human being. He had known for many months now that God wanted him alive for some purpose—but what would there be for him when it came time to die?

14

A Little Black Book

The fighting had stopped, and Zvi was eager to take a look at his homeland. He had a three-day pass in his hand and the country waiting before him. His active tour of army service would soon be over. It was high time he surveyed his surroundings. On this leave, he decided, he would visit the port city of Haifa. This time he would go neither as a prisoner nor as a military conscript—he was strictly a tourist. Three happy days of walking and gawking totally possessed the contented citizen. The spectacular view of the harbor from the side of Mount Carmel awed the young visitor.

The soldier-traveler didn't have a monetary pittance, but he had little need for much money. A nation grateful to her sons who had fought to save her now extended hospitality to those in the military. Hotels offered free rooms and meals to Joshua's modern counterparts. All Zvi need do was walk in with his request for a night's lodging. Israel was coming alive and the mood was sensational.

Everywhere one went he felt the air of optimistic self-assurance. Exhilarating waves of confidence were breaking over the nation that had so recently fought under a question mark. This country was going somewhere—it was good to be aboard for the journey.

Zvi left Haifa with a treasure tucked under his arm. He had picked up a copy of the Bible written in Hebrew. It would, he figured, meet twin needs: First, he could learn the answers to some of his questions about God. Also, it would be a great tool in helping him with his mastery of Hebrew.

Back in Jerusalem, Zvi spent many hours with his new source of instruction. Whenever he could persuade one of his companions to share some tent time assisting him with his reading program, he was a happy man. Soldiers had an abundance of time on their hands now and, consequently, it wasn't difficult to find a temporary tutor.

One afternoon he was puzzling his way through the Psalms, when he came across a statement that brought him to attention: "When my father and my mother forsake me, then the LORD will take me up. Teach me thy way, O LORD, and lead me in a plain path" (Psalm 27:10-11).

"Who said this?" he asked the sabra who

had been chosen teacher for the day.

"King David," said his young comrade. "He was the second king of our nation. It was he who came here and made Jerusalem the royal city of Israel."

"If he was a king, living in a palace, why would he say a thing like this?" Zvi wondered.

"Very simple," said his instructor. "He was a king, yes, but a man with many troubles. He had great enemies from whom he was forced to flee. At one time even his son turned against him. Many of the things he wrote in the Psalms were about his times of trouble."

This David, Zvi concluded, was a man just like him—trouble upon trouble. Maybe he could learn some things from a man who had spent time in the same boat as the maturing Jew from Poland.

Zvi's mother and father had forsaken him, too. Of course, it was something over which they had no control, and he had nothing but love and fond memories for them. Nevertheless, he had known the life of a forsaken waif, alone and surrounded by a host of enemies.

David said that when it had happened to him, the Lord picked him up. Then he asked God to teach him and lead him in a plain path. It seemed astonishing to Zvi that one who lived so long ago could feel exactly as he did now. From now on, he determined, his prayer would be the same—that God would teach him and lead him in a plain path.

"What are you going to do now that you are out of the army?" an officer friend questioned.

"First," responded Zvi, "I must find a place to live. The army has given me a tent to use, but I've lived in enough tents to suit me. Soon, I hope to find a permanent place to stay.

"Then I will look for work. I don't care what I do, just so I find something I can learn to do well."

"It might not be easy to find work immediately," his officer said. "Until people have time to get things going, work will be scarce."

"Never mind about that," answered Zvi. "There is plenty of time ahead. I will wait for something to come along."

Zvi's tent home was something less than palatial. Often, it was difficult to keep up with it. His tent developed a bad habit of blowing away when he was gone during the day. Even at night, when the wind was up, it was not uncommon to find himself awakened by the sound of fluttering canvas descending about him. Winds in Israel, he found, paid little heed to his threats and complaints as he grappled with ropes and tent stakes in the darkness. After a short time, Zvi concluded he was not cut out for the life of a bedouin. If being born a Jew had its problems, at least one of them should not be chasing a tent all over the Middle East. He approached the authorities with a request to be relocated.

"If you don't mind living with three or four others in one room," he was told, "you can go to the settlement at Talpiyot."

"All I am concerned about right now," said the man who needed a good night's sleep, "is that my house doesn't run away while I'm gone."

"I don't think there is much danger of that," answered the smiling official. "I'll arrange for you to get a place there."

Zvi sacked his belongings, folded his errant tent for the last time, and set out for new quarters at Talpiyot. The settlement center was located on the Bethlehem side of Jerusalem. The area had been settled by Jews in 1924. During the recent conflict, it had been squarely in no man's land. From the human standpoint, the camp was as international a situation as one could find on earth. Jews from a host of nations had come to this way station on their way to permanent homes in Israel.

His first observation was that he would not be lonely at Talpiyot. If anything, finding a place to be alone was virtually impossible. Fifteen thousand people were jammed into an area covering no more than a few acres of rock-strewn ground. Zvi was shown to a barrack he was to share with three young immigrants who had recently entered the country from Morocco. His home measured about six by twelve feet, had two windows on each side and an entry door. It resembled a railroad caboose minus the viewing bays and roof extension. The Moroccans, Zvi found, were not the only residents occupying the small room. Red ticks ranged the walls and found the new occupant a particularly tasty morsel to feast on in the night hours.

The stay at Talpiyot was a time for reflection. Often, in the night, Zvi would find himself wandering once again through the streets of Warsaw. Those mental journeys recreated happy days when the family was together and Adolph Hitler had not yet shattered their lives. Zvi frequently thought about the future. Would it be any better than the past had been? Israel was surrounded by enemies who were determined to destroy her. If they should come again, would the Promised Land become another Europe? But dark thoughts died with bright sunrises that found the young immigrant out early tramping the streets of Jerusalem looking for work, searching passing faces, and peering into cluttered shop windows.

A visit from a middle-aged woman was a turning point. Zvi was sitting outside his tiny home when he first caught sight of her. She had come to Talpiyot after he had been there about two months. She was obviously a European. Zvi judged by her looks that she was in her early sixties. The woman carried a bag full of little black books. He was seated outside his barrack home when she came by. As she approached him, Zvi decided to take a guess at her nationality and spoke to her in German. She smiled broadly and returned his greeting. "You were almost correct," she told him. "You only missed it by a short distance. I am from Switzerland." The two of them shared a few minutes of pleasant conversation before she reached into her bag. "I would like to give you a book," she said.

"What kind of book is it?" Zvi asked.

"This is a New Testament written in Hebrew," she answered cheerfully.

"And what is a New Testament?" he queried.

"It is a part of the Bible," she explained. "It will tell you about the Messiah."

He had heard references to the Messiah in his ghetto days in Europe, and by religious Jews in the army. "I have heard something about the Messiah, but know little beyond the name."

"Then this book will answer your questions," the woman told him earnestly. "There is only one stipulation in my giving it to you: you must promise me that you will read it."

"Yes, I will be glad to read it," he promised. "But I must tell you that I don't read Hebrew very well yet."

"Well," said the woman, "just read slowly and ask the Lord to lead you to understand what you read."

Zvi accepted the little black book with words of gratitude.

When the woman had gone, he thought about what she had counseled him to do. "Ask the Lord to lead you to understand what you read." That is what he had read about in the psalm when David asked the Lord to lead him. The woman's words struck a chord in Zvi's spirit.

Zvi had read magazines in the past, and from time to time novels had fallen into his hands. He found, however, little to interest him in those volumes. The Swiss woman's little black book was another story. As the youthful searcher began to work his way slowly through its pages, he found that it breathed with a vibrancy he had never encountered in a book before. Many of the quotations and references were somewhat familiar to him from what he had read in the Hebrew Bible he had picked up in Haifa. This book spoke about many places in Israel that were known to him. The stories and lessons of the gospels began to give him answers to some of his questions, but his snail's pace reading gave rise to a great many more.

Before long his hunger for the content of his most precious possession began to approximate the drive he had long felt to know God. He was faced, each time he picked up his New Testament, with the problem of his difficulty in understanding Hebrew. His lack of any previous exposure to these Scriptures posed another handicap. Furthermore, there was no one known to him who could help explain what he was reading. Still, he applied himself doggedly to his quest to learn what this book had to say.

Zvi had no explanation for the way he felt. Yet he was intensely aware of the fact that this book drew him to it like a magnet. After awhile, he began to leave the busy and distracting atmosphere of the crowded camp to seek out the quiet of the parks in Jerusalem. There he would sit for hours, glued to the book. It was not unusual for him to be made aware of his surroundings by the growing darkness. The lack of adequate light caused him to become conscious of having read his way through an entire afternoon without food or knowledge of the swift passage of time. Frequently, he would pause at some particularly knotty point and think carefully through what he had read.

He was especially struck by the knowledge that the men who surrounded Jesus were simple, working people like himself. They were not, he learned, highly educated men, but rather men who had a real hunger to learn about the ways of God. He observed that these men were like people of his day, when he read of the times they displayed fear, jealousy, and selfishness. When they rose to honorable exploits or said wonderful things, Zvi would silently cheer them along.

Central in his thoughts, however, was Jesus. The woman had told him this book would speak to him about the Messiah. It did not take long for him to recognize who his little book identified as that distinguished personage. Jesus of Nazareth intrigued him. He was thoroughly captivated by the unfolding of the Carpenter's life on the pages before him. Zvi lingered over passages that recorded what Jesus said and did. He was moved by the realization that simple, sick, and hungry people could always approach Him and get a sympathetic response. When he read of how Jesus had raised Lazarus from the dead and returned him to his sisters, he thought of his feelings about his friend David and his mourning father.

Above everything else, he was impressed with the troubles encountered by Jesus.

This Man did nothing but good, yet some men hated and opposed Him. Later they succeeded in nailing Him to a cross. He found great difficulty in comprehending why this would happen. When he considered it carefully, he thought about how his own people, and he, himself, had suffered without a reason.

One afternoon, he was seated on his bed in the barrack at Talpiot reading his New Testament when a friend came by to see him. "What are you reading?" the visitor inquired.

"It is part of the Bible," Zvi answered.

"I did not know you were a religious Jew," his friend observed.

"I can't say that I am a religious Jew," Zvi said, "but neither can I say I am not religious. This book says many good things to me, things that I don't know how to understand yet. But I can say these things interest me very much."

"This Bible you are reading, is it the Torah?" the man wanted to know.

"No," Zvi replied, "it is the New Testament."

"That is not a book for Jews," the friend warned. "It is just fairy tales and bluffs made up by Christians."

Zvi was puzzled. "I have read this book for many days now, and I admit that there is much about it I do not understand, but I have not read anything that has done me harm or caused me to want to become a bad person. I have read only good things in this book."

"If you are smart, you will take my advice and get rid of that book," his advisor stated firmly.

"I cannot bring myself to believe it will do me any harm," Zvi answered.

His friend went away shaking his head. Zvi watched him go and wondered why the man felt as he did. He was obviously very much opposed to the book—but why? Jesus himself had been a good Jew. As a matter of fact, Zvi thought, there had never been as great a Jew on earth as this One. Why then should he, another Jew, not read about Him? He did not know how to reply to the things he had been told; he knew only that what he had read was finding a lodging place in his soul.

Periodic opportunities for work were beginning to open to him now, and he selected the building trade for his permanent vocation. Zvi learned quickly and worked very hard. It did not matter to him what the task involved. He would do anything that afforded him a good chance to do an honest day's work. Men who were in the contracting business soon learned the name of the rock-hard immigrant from Poland who was ready to handle the toughest jobs they had.

Wherever he went and whatever he was doing, Zvi's little black book was with him. He was afraid to leave it behind in his room for fear someone would take it. If he had a few minutes off or was out of work for a few days, he could be found off to himself carefully pursuing the open pages before him.

15

Dare I Enter?

Few men have approached a spiritual confrontation with God weighed down by more obvious disadvantages than Zvi Weichert. Death, privation, and a recurring cycle of cruel disappointments had buffeted him during his childhood and youth. As a boy, he had looked out on a world intent on his destruction. While he clawed and fought to stay alive, his path took him from one tragic revelation to another. Zvi had seen degenerate humanity with its teeth bared and hands reddened with the blood of innocents. He had weathered a storm of demonic brutality that defied analysis by sane minds. Bitterness, persecutions and degrading meanness, inhuman cruelty, frustration, and fear were among the ingredients that boiled about him in the seething cauldron into which he had been plunged. By all standards of human computation, it should have destroyed him—it did not.

Conversely, and ironically, a few men

have entered a personal period of spiritual crisis with more obvious openness than did Zvi Weichert. He did not carry with him the inherited prejudices of Judaism or Christianity. From the spiritual standpoint, Zvi had been brought along in a near vacuum. Satanic manifestations had swirled about him throughout his life. While he could not provide precise theological definitions for what he was caught up in, he could certainly acknowledge the reality of the experience. When it came to God, however, he was confronted by a void. His knowledge was so limited that it could be properly described as nonexistent.

There had been one fact available to his mental and spiritual facilities of which he was certain: he was a Jew. The force of that knowledge had been with him throughout the years of his suffering. When he surfaced in Poland after the war, it never occurred to him to attempt to hide his identity and forsake his race. His physical features and identification papers would have made it an easy matter for him to have done so. Being a Jew had stigmatized him to a point that rebellion against his past could easily have afflicted him. Members of his family were all dead, and the future for Jews in Europe was bleak. But Zvi was never seriously tempted to turn his back on his own people. Furthermore, as if he were drawn by some mysterious inner mechanism, he had gravitated toward Israel. When he arrived in the land of his fathers, he knew instinctively that he was at home and among his own people.

From that point on, Zvi began to move through a succession of steps that brought him to the threshold of decision. The knowledge of his being alone in the world had left him empty—and he was acutely aware of the painful void. At Latrun, he had frankly faced himself and acknowledged that God existed and cared for him. Thus, he awakened to spiritual reality as a hungry young man. In Haifa he had received his first exposure to the foundational portion of the Word of God. Through reading the Scriptures, he identified with Jehovah and His ability to speak to the needs of his fathers in days gone by as well as to his personal needs centuries later. Then he had received his copy of the Scriptural component that would rest securely upon the foundation and complete the structure—the New Testament.

As one views the whole he can construct, mentally, a providential pyramid—one that moved from base to point in stages, drawing him upward to the pinnacle that unerringly directed him toward the One who could satisfy the hunger that throbbed within him.

Without a hand to guide him or a human voice to counsel him, he stayed close to the New Testament, which he somehow knew held the answer to his longings. Day after day he soaked up its truths, until he came to the place of direct personal confrontation — he felt he had to do something about what he had learned. As he read the Bible, he came to grips with the matter of his need to be a justified man, not merely a religious practitioner. He began to understand, through his reading, that it was necessary for the Messiah to suffer for the sins of the people before Zvi, or anyone else, could approach God. He had wondered, when he read the accounts of the animal sacrifices of ancient days, what could be offered to make peace for him today. When he found that the Messiah had occupied the place of the slain lamb once for all, he began to see that the answer to his quest was bound up in the Messiah, who had borne the sins of mankind.

Zvi did not see the Old and New Testaments as isolated entities, separate and opposed to one another, but as a complementary unit, the one being the logical extension of the other. Each was incomplete without the addition of its counterpart.

Many questions pressed upon his mind in those days, but one began to predominate: How could he find the peace that Jesus promised His followers?

It was a sunny Wednesday evening as Zvi was returning from his day's work in Jerusalem. As he often did in those days, he spent some time sitting in the park engrossed in reading his black book and mulling over the passages before him. The dinner hour had already passed when he decided to go up the street to a small restaurant he had seen, and eat before returning to Talpiyot. As he passed a small building, he could hear the sound of people who were lifting hearty voices in song. The words that came to his ears were from a hymn about the person of whom he had been reading, Jesus. Although it was not obvious from the external appearance of the building, he knew it must be a meeting of believers in Christ as Messiah. He had never attended such a service, so he was not familiar with how they conducted worship. Whatever it was, they certainly sounded happy about it. When he came back from the restaurant, a few people still lingered around the front of the building with Bibles tucked under their arms. Zvi fingered the New Testament he carried in his pocket and felt an urge to stop and talk with them, but did not give in to it.

For the next few evenings, he arranged his routine so he would be in that vicinity at about the same time. He saw no life about the place until Sunday night, when, once again, he saw people filing into the building. He walked by the front of the meeting house a couple of times during the service but did not venture inside.

Later he sat in the park and thought it over. He wanted to go inside and see for himself what went on, but he was hesitant. "Dare I enter?" he asked himself. "What if they chase me away and tell me they don't want me to come there? But why should I be afraid?" he concluded. He had certainly been chased away from enough places in his lifetime. If they didn't want him, he would leave.

He left work the following Wednesday evening, anxious to get to his destination on time. After dinner at the restaurant, he walked up the street and turned in at the entrance to the church. Zvi felt very self-conscious as he stepped toward the door. He did not know quite what to expect. His fears would be put to rest quickly. Instead of a stone, an outstretched hand came his way. The man was smiling and extending a warm welcome to the newcomer. Zvi entered and took a seat on one of the benches near the front of the building.

He took a few minutes to look around the small auditorium. It was a simple setting. Across the front was a table with a good-sized menorah in the center of it. On the opposite side of the room sat a worn piano.

A small lectern was positioned between the two pieces of furniture. Two men and a woman were talking together and looking at a book like the one he saw in the rack attached to the seat in front of him.

One by one, the people came into the building, nodding to him cordially as they found their seats. Promptly at 7:30 one of the men rose and walked to the lectern. The man announced a hymn, and everyone reached for one of the books. Zvi was interested to find that the book was filled with songs written in Hebrew. Suddenly, he became aware of the fact that everyone else was standing. He could feel his face flush as he scrambled to his feet. The service had barely started, and he had already made one mistake. He decided he would observe carefully from now on so he would not be caught sitting again when he should be standing. After the song was finished, the leader called on one of the men in the congregation to pray. Zvi saw that the people dropped their chins to their chests and closed their eyes as the man addressed the Lord.

After more hymn singing, the man announced the services on the following Sunday and talked about people who were sick or needy, asking those present to pray for them. When he had concluded, another man came to the speaker's stand and laid his

Bible upon it. The people were instructed to open their Bibles to the seventeenth chapter of the gospel of John. Zvi looked about to see men and women eagerly thumbing through the pages of their Bibles to find the passage. It dawned on him that he, too, could participate in this part of the service. He reached in his pocket, drew out his well-worn Testament and began leafing through the pages to find the place the speaker had announced.

The words the man read were familiar to Zvi, and it pleased him to be able to follow the reading. He was also impressed when he realized that this was the first time he had heard the Bible read aloud. Reading to an audible accompaniment established a feeling of kinship with the people who had come to the meeting.

The pastor spoke at length about the verses, which told of Jesus' prayer for the disciples. The man dwelt on the Lord's love and concern for His people; how He would meet their needs and answer prayer. "Any believer in the Messiah," he said, "could come at any time and talk with the Lord, and the Father would hear him and answer his prayer." Zvi listened with an intensity that was mirrored vividly on his face. When the man finished speaking, he wanted him to go on. It seemed to him that the man had just begun when he stopped. *Oh well,* he thought, *there will be another time*. He resolved to return for the next meeting.

Several people came up to introduce themselves when the meeting was over. They were friendly and invited him to come back again. At the door, Zvi had a question for the pastor: "Do you meet every week at this time?"

"Yes, and we meet on Sundays as well. I hope you will be back to meet with us again.

"By the way, I didn't introduce myself, I am Moshe Kaplan."

The man shook Zvi's hand, as he responded to the introduction with his name.

On the walk home, he thought about the things the pastor had discussed during the meeting. All in all, it was an impressive experience. He was anxious for Sunday to come so he could go back for a worship service.

Sunday's message was different from the one he had heard on Wednesday night. Mr. Kaplan spoke on Jesus as the sin-bearer, One who came as a substitute and took the sins of the people on Himself, to make it possible for men and women to be saved from their sins. "Men," he said, "must turn from their sins and accept what the Messiah has done for them. We must be delivered from our sins by the sacrifice provided by the Messiah, Jesus."

The talk squared with the general conception Zvi had formed in his mind regarding the Messiah. He would come again and hear more of what this man had to say about the Book.

For the next several Wednesdays and Sundays he came faithfully to the services. His eager ears soaked up every word that fell from the preacher's lips. He was even croaking out the songs as the people sang together.

Then one Wednesday night Zvi left the service with a feeling of depression. He couldn't understand what was happening to him. The talk had been interesting, and he had agreed with what he had heard. Why, then, should he feel as he did? All the way home he turned it over in his mind. It was as if a weight had been placed on him that must somehow be removed.

When he arrived as his barrack in Talpiyot, he was still a troubled young man. He lay for awhile listening to the heavy breathing of his sleeping companions. Zvi was far removed from the embrace that had so often taken him beyond the troubles of his waking world. Tonight, sleep would not come to shut down his whirring mind, even temporarily.

Slowly it came to him. He needed to do something about what he had heard and read—Zvi needed to be saved from his sin.

That was it! That was what had made him feel so miserable. For weeks he had heard about the Messiah—words that agreed perfectly with what he had read in the Bible—but he had not done anything about it himself. He vowed, there in the darkness, that he would speak to the pastor about it on Wednesday night after the service.

"Can I talk with you after the meeting tonight?" Zvi asked Mr. Kaplan.

"Why certainly, Zvi, I would be happy for us to spend some time together."

When the service had ended, Zvi approached the speaker.

"It's a long story," the young man began, "but what it comes down to is this: I want you to explain to me what I have to do to be saved."

"Well," said the pastor, "I would be delighted to tell you what you need to do. But I want you first to know, Zvi, that this is a very serious matter, one which a person does not undertake lightly."

"Yes, I am aware of that," Zvi answered. "I have been thinking about it for a long time. Now I know it is what I have been searching for but did not know how to find it. I must find peace with God, and I know it can be found only through the Messiah."

"Here is a point that you must understand," counseled the pastor. "If you accept Jesus as your Messiah and Savior, you will be in for trouble. It is very difficult for people to live openly for Christ here in Israel these days. It may be necessary for you to endure suffering if you become His follower.

"For that reason, you must be very sure that this is your decision and not one you have been talked into by me or anyone else. In other words, you must be absolutely convinced that this is what you want to do."

Zvi answered thoughtfully, "Mr. Kaplan, the reason I came here in the first place was that I was searching for answers to questions I had in my life and ones that had come to me from the book. I am very sure that this is what I want to do. As far as the suffering goes, I have read about how much He suffered for me. It will be a privilege to be allowed to suffer for Him."

"Good. Now the next question is this: Do you believe in Jesus as the Messiah and are you willing to accept Him as your Savior and Lord?"

"Yes—yes! Without any question," said Zvi, "I am convinced that He is the Messiah and my Savior."

The two men prayed together, and the simple transaction was completed— simple, yet profound beyond anything that can be computed or communicated through human phraseology. Zvi Weichert, survivor of the Holocaust, had experienced the new birth. Since boyhood, he had longed for and sought after a new beginning. Now he had found it. He was a new creation in Jesus the Messiah. Zvi knew that this was the point to which God had been leading him through all these years. Even when he was blind and completely ignorant of spiritual realities, the Lord was patiently protecting him, providing for him, and leading him along the way to bring him to this place. How good God had been to suffer with him this long and now give him eternal life!

Zvi would attempt to analyze the results of his climactic encounter with the Messiah. It crystalized into two identifiable categories: peace and joy. The void in his life had been filled. All that had been left vacant through all the tragedies that had beset him, had been occupied by the entrance of the Messiah-Savior. He was no longer at war with God or his past; he had made his peace with Jehovah. A joy possessed him that he could hardly contain. He did not believe it was possible for anyone to experience the kind of happiness that was now flooding his being. He had never known it in any measure before he found it that night in a simple building in Jerusalem. It was, he would find, a joy that would not diminish with the passing years.

At long last Zvi found his safe haven. There in Jerusalem, City of Peace, he had found rest in the Prince of Peace. Jerusalem would continue to be his earthly home; Jesus would remain his eternal refuge.

Epilogue

You may be wondering what became of this extraordinary man after we left him at the threshold of the fifties.

Well, I can tell you that Zvi is alive and very much in the mainstream of life in his chosen land.

He has served with distinction in the Israeli Defense Forces. Zvi has fought in all of Israel's wars for survival. He continues currently as a member of the reserve and does regular tours of duty with the army.

Today Zvi lives in Jerusalem near the scenes he shared with us across these pages. He is married to a gracious Persian Jewess, also a believer in Christ, who, over the years has presented her beaming husband with three fine sons and one lovely daughter. Her name, appropriately, is Ruth. You will remember that Zvi's European family included three boys and a girl. This seems to be one of the many ways through which the Lord has balanced the scale for Zvi.

And what about Zvi's faith in Jesus Christ? Did it last? To say yes is almost an understatement. It is, assuredly, an inadequate response. Zvi's testimony for his Messiah has radiated with steadily increasing brilliance across the decades. His is a rare mix of boldness, compassion, and sensitivity that has won respect for his witness and gives him opportunities for ministry among Israelis from all walks of life.

But that is another story. Perhaps we'll tell it someday.

Elwood McQuaid

Moody Press, a ministry of the Moody Bible Institute, is designed for education, evangelization, and edification.